ST PANCRAS
INTERNATIONAL

ST PANCRAS
INTERNATIONAL

150 FOR 150
FACTS YEARS

The
History
Press

The facts in this book started life as 192 images that were sourced and annotated by the UCL History students listed below, as part of a St Pancras International 150th Anniversary Research Project commissioned by HS1.

Sara Ali, Alicia Alli, Nick Bailey, Susannah Bain, Ayesha Baloch, Genevieve Caulfield, Xiyu Cheng, Matthew Dawe, Emma Dove, Cholé Ducroizet-Boitaud, Peter Fitzsimons, Alexander Freeland, Scarlet Furness, Caitlin John, Michael Johnson, Christiana Karagiorgi, Hannah Keen, Michael Launchbury, Imran Loades Dhalla, Risha Patel, Caycee Peskett-Hill, Eliza Riley-Smith, Sian Robbins, Jamie Sillitoe, Huw Steer, James Stockham, Kevin Tailor, Isobel Thompson, Holly Todd and Elle Zacharia under the supervision and with editorial assistance from Dr Chris Jeppesen and Professor Margot Finn.

Archive image research by Cate Ludlow.

First published 2018

The History Press
The Mill, Brimscombe Port
Stroud, Gloucestershire, GL5 2QG
www.thehistorypress.co.uk

British Library Cataloguing in Publication Data.
A catalogue record for this book is available from the British Library.

ISBN 978 0 7509 8781 3

Typesetting and origination by The History Press
Printed in Turkey by Imak

ST PANCRAS
INTERNATIONAL

150 FOR 150
FACTS YEARS

The History Press

The facts in this book started life as 192 images that were sourced and
annotated by the UCL History students listed below, as part of a
St Pancras International 150th Anniversary Research Project commissioned by HS1.

Sara Ali, Alicia Alli, Nick Bailey, Susannah Bain, Ayesha Baloch, Gen-
evieve Caulfield, Xiyu Cheng, Matthew Dawe, Emma Dove, Cholé
Ducroizet-Boitaud, Peter Fitzsimons, Alexander Freeland, Scarlet
Furness, Caitlin John, Michael Johnson, Christiana Karagiorgi, Hannah
Keen, Michael Launchbury, Imran Loades Dhalla, Risha Patel, Caycee
Peskett-Hill, Eliza Riley-Smith, Sian Robbins, Jamie Sillitoe, Huw
Steer, James Stockham, Kevin Tailor, Isobel Thompson, Holly Todd and
Elle Zacharia under the supervision and with editorial assistance from
Dr Chris Jeppesen and Professor Margot Finn.

Archive image research by Cate Ludlow.

First published 2018

The History Press
The Mill, Brimscombe Port
Stroud, Gloucestershire, GL5 2QG
www.thehistorypress.co.uk

Typesetting and origination by The History Press
Printed in Turkey by Imak

CONTENTS

INTRODUCTION

ST PANCRAS STATION was opened in 1868 and is one of the wonders of Victorian engineering, the centrepiece for the vibrant borough it inhabits. Along with the former Midland Grand Hotel, the station is a masterpiece of Victorian Gothic architecture and one of the most elegant in the world. In honour of its 150th anniversary, HS1 commissioned UCL to collate historical information relating to the history of the station and its surrounding area, here re-worked into an easy-to-digest illustrated fact book. Did you know there was once a farm in the heart of the St Pancras parish area? Or why Midland Railway built a special viaduct to travel over St Pancras? Read on to find out ...

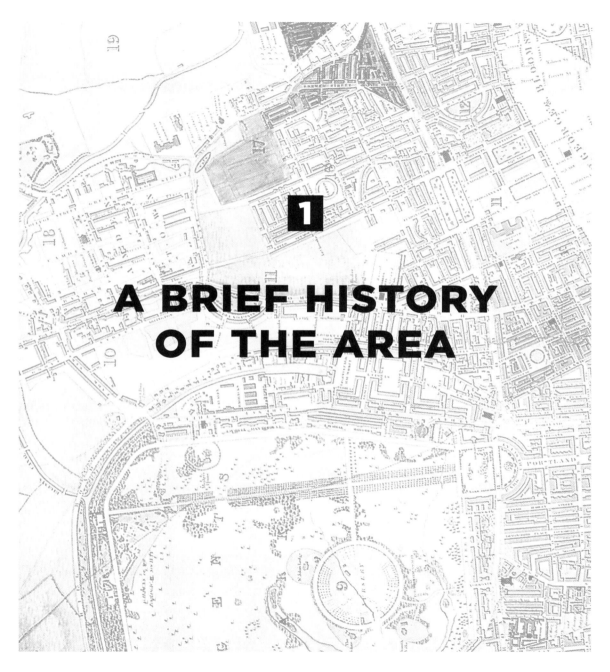

1

A BRIEF HISTORY
OF THE AREA

1   The St Pancras area in Georgian times was almost entirely rural

Map of St Pancras in 1833. (Wellcome Library, London)

Contemporary maps show little to suggest the urban transformation that this area would undergo over the next 150 years. The opening of the New Road (present-day Euston Road) in 1756 began to change this. Initially built to reduce the volume of traffic passing through Westminster and the City of London as farmers took their livestock to market at Smithfields, as well as to ensure troops could be moved quickly around the city in case of emergency, the fields along the New Road soon began to be developed as sites of light industry, brick yards or refuse dumps. Over the next fifty years, growing numbers of wealthy Londoners looked to escape the overcrowded centre for less populated areas, with plenty of open land and clean air. This initiated a house-building boom that pushed the city northwards into the area around St Pancras. In the 1770s, the population of St Pancras was still under 1,000, but by the turn of the nineteenth century it had risen to 31,779, as new arrivals streamed into Somers Town and Camden Town. Gradually the area's rural landscape disappeared as St Pancras was increasingly integrated into a constantly expanding city. London's population reached 1 million people by 1800 and 100 years later numbered over 6 million.

2   There was once a farm in the heart of the St Pancras parish area

Built in 1776, Capper's Farm House remained a well-known local landmark until the early twentieth century. It was named after Christopher Capper, 'a great cow keeper' who had farmed and grazed cows for milk in St Pancras parish since 1693. His daughters subsequently gained notorious reputations in the area as 'two old maiden sisters': one used to ride with shears to cut the strings of kites flown by little boys, whilst the second sister reportedly stole the clothes of boys who trespassed on their land to bathe. During the 1840s, Capper's Farm was purchased by the Heal family. Despite a change in the ownership, the Heals were required to accommodate forty cows that remained on the land, something that became increasingly difficult as London sprawled outwards. Capper's Farm House survived until 1913, when it was torn down to make room for the expanding Heal & Son furniture business. The development of the Capper's Farm land and the farmhouse's eventual destruction offers an important insight into nineteenth-century urbanisation and the changing economy of the local area from its agricultural roots in the eighteenth century. These socio-economic changes resulted in the eradication of the rural economy from the Tottenham Court Road area, to be replaced with the dense urban thoroughfare seen today.

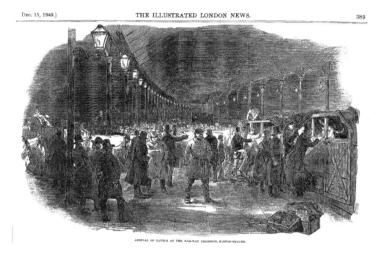

Cattle arriving at nearby Euston rail terminus in 1849. A whole herd was once kept in the heart of St Pancras. (Wellcome Library, London)

School, church and parsonage at Agar Town, London. Wood engraving by W. E. Hodgkin, 1858. The cottages were nearby. (Wellcome Library, London)

3   Agar Town cottage residents opposed railway construction

Despite contemporary criticism, and its subsequent repetition by later historians, that Agar Town was little more than, in the words of Charles Dickens, an 'English Connemara', the reality was more complex. Historian Steven Denford highlights the dangers of relying entirely on nineteenth-century sources that give no voice to local inhabitants. In place of the prevailing stereotype, his research has revealed an area and community that, whilst poor, contained a greater diversity of people than frequently suggested. Contrary to the entrenched stereotype, relatively few Irish migrants or unemployed are listed on the census returns of those living in Agar Town in the 1850s and '60s; the majority of residents are listed as working craftsmen or labourers. Most houses in the area were occupied by a single family, rather than being subdivided, and were rented. This meant, however, that few occupants were entitled to compensation once the Midland Railway Company started purchasing land, leases, and property from landowners or the parish authorities. Despite efforts by the local community to use the courts to stop the construction of the railway, they were ultimately unsuccessful. Even so, this opposition did increase the cost of construction considerably for the Midland Railway Company. The labourers' rows of cottages were situated on the edge of Agar Town, next to St Pancras Old Church.

4 Dr Jenner pioneered his revolutionary treatment at St Pancras Smallpox Hospital

'Variolation' – the deliberate introduction of matter from smallpox pustules into a healthy patient's skin in the hope that a mild infection would ultimately protect against a more serious attack – had been introduced to Britain from the Ottoman empire in the 1720s; however, this had proved unpopular with patients. Edward Jenner's research suggested an alternative approach by revealing that those who had suffered from cowpox would not contract the more dangerous smallpox. Jenner's method involved transferring infected matter into a cut on the patient's arm; the method came to form the basis of modern vaccination.

From 1793 until the 1840s, the St Pancras Smallpox Hospital occupied the area adjacent to the present-day station, now the site of King's Cross. A smallpox hospital had first opened in 1743 at nearby Battle Bridge, but when this proved insufficient for the number of patients, the hospital moved here. When the Great Northern Railway Company demolished it to make way for the new station in the 1840s, the hospital relocated again to Highgate. As well as caring for those suffering from the disease, the hospital's chief physician, Dr William Woodville, was a keen supporter of Jenner and allowed him to refine his vaccination technique on his patients. Nevertheless, the government did not introduce a compulsory programme of vaccination until the 1850s and the disease remained endemic in Britain into the late nineteenth century, with over 70,000 dying of smallpox in 1870 alone. As the admissions records of the St Pancras Hospital illustrate, the disease remained most devastating amongst London's poorer communities, like those living around Somers Town.

Opposite: Caricature of vaccination scene at the Smallpox and Inoculation Hospital at St Pancras by James Gillary, 1802. (Library of Congress, LC-USZC4-3147)

VACCINE POCK hot from ye COW

J. Gillray, del. & ft.

5   The Piccadilly Line is built on land once belonging to the Foundling Hospital

Established in 1739, the Foundling Hospital was one of St Pancras and Bloomsbury's most famous institutions and largest landowners throughout the nineteenth century. Founded by Thomas Coram, it served as a home and hospital to abandoned and orphaned children. As the underground rail network spread across London during the late nineteenth and early twentieth centuries, rail companies required land to construct tunnels and stations. A deed transferred land from the Foundling Hospital to the Great Northern Piccadilly & Brompton Railway Co., later forming the Piccadilly Line. The company took an area in Bloomsbury where the company would 'maintain and use the tunnels constructed according to the levels indicated in such last mentioned sectional plan' as the line ran south from King's Cross St Pancras. The Great Northern Piccadilly & Brompton Railway Underground line opened in 1906, serving twenty-two stations over 14.17km, with three of the stations situated in the St Pancras area.

6   St Pancras Hospital was once a workhouse

Situated next to St Pancras junction, St Pancras Hospital, which specialises in geriatric and psychiatric care, now occupies the building that used to be the borough's workhouse. Over the years, it has served as a psychiatric unit and as a geriatric hospital, but in 1951 it became the home of the first School of Hospital Catering. Funded by the King's Fund, which had long been concerned with 'the cause of good feeding' in hospitals, the school trained hospital chefs to work in the newly formed National Health Service. When the NHS began in 1948, F. Avery Jones, Chairman of the Fund's Hospital Catering and Diet Committee, lamented the 'system of archaic kitchens' in British hospitals. In preparation for the opening of the school, the kitchens at St Pancras hospital were renovated through an £11,000 grant from the Fund. The primary function was the provision of refresher courses to those presently employed as hospital catering staff, but the school also offered bursaries to fully train individuals as catering officers. Upon the school's opening, the Duke of Gloucester, a patron of the King's Fund, described it as 'breaking new ground'. The school's chef instructor was H.C. Jupp.

7   St Pancras's Victorian almshouses still stand as housing

Although housing provision and living conditions have improved over the course of the twentieth century, these remain deeply contentious issues, especially as the threat of redevelopment and gentrification threaten to displace the local community once more. Before Greenswood Almshouses in Rousden Street were renovated by the St Pancras Housing Association in 1984, the area's Victorian housing was in a run-down state. Originally built in 1840, by the 1980s the building had fallen into a state of total disrepair despite, in theory, still being intended to provide housing for elderly residents. The St Pancras Housing Association asked the architectural practice Peter Mishcon & Associates to undertake the task of renovating the building, for which the firm won third prize in the *Times*/RICS Conservation Award. The almshouses are now run by Harrison Housing and currently provide housing to elderly women.

8   The 'Brill' market in Somers Town sold tea from India

Products at the Brill included Assam tea from India, fresh bread, and gin. Although much of the area was demolished to make way for the Midland Railway, Edward Walford described the atmosphere in his account of the Brill in *Old and New London*, written in 1878:

Brill Row, at the northern end of Skinner Street, together with the 'Brill' tavern close by, are nearly all that remains of the locality once familiarly known by that name, which was nothing more nor less than a range of narrow streets crossing each other at right angles, and full of costermongers' shops and barrows, but which were swept away during the formation of the Midland Railway Terminus ... As the philanthropic or curious visitor enters Skinner Street, about eleven o'clock some bright Sunday morning, his ears will be greeted, not by the barking of dogs and the roaring of infuriated bulls, as of old, but by the unnaturally loud cries of men, women, boys, and girls, anxious to sell edibles and drinkables – in fact, everything which a hard-working man or poor sempstress is supposed to need in order to keep body and soul together. The various so-called necessaries of life have here their special advocates. The well-known 'buy, buy, buy,' has, at the 'Brill,' a peculiar shrillness of tone, passing often into a scream – and well it may, for the meat is all ticketed at 4½d. per pound. Here the female purchasers are not generally styled 'ladies,' but 'women,' and somewhat after this fashion – 'This is the sort of cabbage, or meat, or potatoes to buy, women'; and each salesman seems to think that his success depends upon the loudness of his cry ... The purchasers not only come from all parts of Somers Town itself to this spot on a Sunday morning, but from Camden Town, Holloway, Hampstead, and Highgate, and even from distances of five and six miles. The leading impression made by the moving scene is that of great activity and an 'eye to business.' Everyone at the 'Brill,' as a rule, comes there on a Sunday morning for a definite purpose. The women come to buy meat, fish, vegetables, and crockery; and the men, chiefly 'navigators,' as they are termed, come to purchase boots, boot-laces, blouses, trousers, coats, caps, and other articles of wearing apparel. Altogether, at the Brill matters are carried on in a business-like way. The salesmen, many of them young boys, are too intent on selling, and the purchasers too intent on buying, to warrant the supposition that they derive much spiritual benefit from the preachers of all persuasions and of no persuasions who frequent the neighbourhood. The most ardent, and apparently the most successful, of the street preachers are those who occupy posts in the immediate vicinity, and 'hold forth' in familiar strains on the advantages of teetotalism, and the evil consequences following intemperance.

9   The St Pancras area was once home to one of the biggest markets in London

Chalton Street remained Somers Town's main shopping thoroughfare throughout the late nineteenth and first half of the twentieth century. Major markets often grew up around railway stations due to the easy supply of fresh food and produce. Chalton Street's bustling market comprised around 300 traders, one of the busiest in London, and a wide variety of shops, including the grocer's J. Sainsbury at Nos 86–87, a Hovis baker's shop, Peark's Stores 'For Value', Western's Laundries, L. Rose Boot & Shoe Maker, and Parry's Haircutters & Shaving Salon. The street was also known for its pubs, including the Cock Tavern and Somers Town Coffee House, and cafes like P. Tennison served such delights as stewed eels and mashed potato. Following damage during the Blitz, the area has undergone extensive redevelopment. Some former residents have lamented the loss of community that the market was seen to foster, recalling with pleasure the diversity of accents heard around the shops and stalls. Over the last decade the Somers Town Festival of Cultures has taken place in Chalton Street, once again celebrating the local area's identity.

10   Female pupils in Cromer Street did British military exercises

In 1906, female pupils at Cromer Street School participated in a popular form of early-twentieth century exercise: 'Indian clubs'. The exercise routine had been introduced to Britain by military personnel returning from India, where they used the weighted clubs (which actually originated in Persia) to strengthen arm muscles and improve agility. Beginners were advised to start with clubs weighing 2–3lb and only to progress to heavier clubs once they had perfected the swinging technique. The popularity of the Indian clubs at this time transcended gender lines, with men, women and children engaging in the exercise, including during school PE lessons. The Indian clubs even appeared as a gymnastic event in both the 1904 and 1932 Olympic Games.

11   St Pancras is named after a 14-year-old Roman martyr

St Pancras Old Church has been an anchor amongst the changing tides of religious practice in London. Like the parish it serves, it is named in recognition of a 14-year-old Roman martyr, beheaded for his Christian faith in AD 304. Debate remains over the origins of the church itself; some claim a church has stood in this location since AD 314, whilst others have dated its origin from a sixth-century altar stone. The church's rich layered history was revealed during its renovation in 1848, from when the building seen today dates. Norman materials and designs were found within its walls, as well as items marking the turbulent upheavals of the sixteenth-century Reformation. Despite the encroachment of the railway during the 1860s, St Pancras Old Church proved a durable and important institution in the lives of Somers Town's rapidly growing population. Today it remains a lively and dedicated institution, which as well as continuing to provide religious service also hosts concerts and other social events, and has been described by *Time Out* as 'London's most spectacular intimate venue'.

South view of the Church of St Pancras. (Wellcome Library, London)

12   Immigrants to the St Pancras area included refugees from the French Revolution

Ever since the area was first developed in the late eighteenth century, Somers Town has had a diverse and eclectic population. Early arrivals included refugees from Europe's religious wars and those fleeing the French Revolution, while the mid-nineteenth century saw large numbers of Irish migrants arrive, many of whom worked on the construction of the railways. Since the 1950s, the community living around Somers Town and St Pancras has undergone further change as new migrant communities from around the world have settled in the area. One newspaper report from the early 1960s described St Pancras as having 'a lively, quick tongued population. They have many of the East Ender's characteristics but the strong peppering of Greek, Irish, and Latin residents gives St Pancras a peculiarly individual tang.' These decades also saw arrivals from South Asia and the Caribbean, many of whom found jobs in London's expanding economy, and more recently the area has seen the growth of East African and Eastern European communities.

Contemporary print of the French Revolution by Scottish artist Isaac Cruikshank. Many Parisians fleeing the violence came to London. (Library of Congress, LC-USZC2-3597)

13   Shakespeare's editor is buried in St Pancras Old Church

The Illustrated London News took a keen interest in the progress of construction as the Midland Railway approached St Pancras, providing readers with an etching of workmen exhuming bodies as the railway passed across the burial grounds of St Giles and St Pancras Old Church in 1866. The Midland Railway Company had had to apply to Parliament for permission to cut across the burial grounds, which was granted on condition that the exhumations were done with care and the coffins reburied elsewhere. In the event, however, the bodies were carelessly thrown about and bones muddled together. With public outcry mounting, *The Illustrated London News* reported the 'foetid' conditions on the construction site. Ultimately, construction continued unabated, albeit under tighter supervision. Anger lingered after the completion of the railway, however, with Frederick Miller recording in his 1874 book, *Saint Pancras, Past and Present*: 'In 1866 the work of desecration commenced … The Railway is no respecter of persons living or dead.'

Shakespeare's portrait in his First Folio, published posthumously. (British Library, G.11631, title page)

Among those buried in the cemetery were the philosopher and writer Mary Wollstonecraft and her husband William Godwin, the parents of Mary Shelley; Lewis Theobald, editor to Shakespeare; and it is likely that Charles Dicken's younger sister was also buried there.

St Pancras Old Church. (Pete via WikimediaCommons, CC2.0)

14   Thomas Hardy has a tree named after him in St Pancras churchyard

In the 1960s, the Hardy Tree in Old St Pancras churchyard was surrounded by gravestones. The stones were moved during the construction of the Midland Line in the 1860s, when a section of the graveyard had to be dug up and the bodies exhumed. Before he achieved fame as a writer, Thomas Hardy had been an architect's assistant and responsible for overseeing the removal of the bodies. These stones commemorate some of the yard's more notable figures and were clustered in a circle with an ash tree planted at the centre. The tree has subsequently been given Hardy's name.

15   Charles Dickens lived in Somers Town

Situated to the west of St Pancras stands the area of Somers Town, where the Midland Railway Goods Depot was built in the 1880s. Somers Town was first developed in the 1780s on largely rural land with the intention of capitalising on the building boom that was bringing wealthy residents north away from the crowded centres of the City of London and Westminster. However, fashionable society ultimately moved further west instead, with many of the arrivals in late eighteenth-century Somers Town coming from France as refugees fleeing the

Charles Dickens. (Library of Congress, LC-USZ61-694)

violence of the revolution. Subsequent dips in the housing market in the 1820s led to much of the stock being sold off cheap or subdivided for private rent. By the mid-nineteenth century residents tended to come from the lower middle and 'respectable' working classes, including Charles Dickens, who lived in The Polygon in the 1820s. With the coming of the railway, however, overcrowding became more of a problem as many of the residents forced from their homes in Agar Town relocated to nearby streets.

16   Somers Town workers in the Victorian era often faced 'wretched' conditions

George Godwin began his career as an architect, and later became editor of the magazine *The Builder* in 1844. In this role, he campaigned vigorously for greater government intervention to improve sanitary and housing conditions in 'slum areas'. In 1864, he published *Another Blow for Life,* using the interior of a mid-Victorian shoemaker's workshop in Somers Town to illustrate the cramped and poorly-ventilated working conditions faced by artisans in London and to lament the lack of interest, from both elites and the poor themselves, in improving standards. Godwin conjured a bleak picture of the craftsmen's world: '[in] wretched apartments in an ill-drained house may be found men and boys huddled together without room to breathe; where, as one so placed remarked grimly, while they are drawing the strings of misery, they are "closing up" their own lives.'

While Somers Town was never a centre of the heavy industry so often associated with the industrial revolution, its proximity to Regent's Canal and subsequently several railway termini meant that light industry did develop, employing both skilled artisans and more general labour. As more people moved into the area and the railway occupied more land, overcrowding became an increasing problem, which Godwin used to demand better provision for those displaced by the railway.

Opposite: Godwin's Somers Town illustration from *Another Blow for Life* (1864). (Wellcome Library, London)

17 The eastern edge of the St Pancras area was originally a giant rubbish dump

The arrival of the Midland Railway and construction of St Pancras station dramatically transformed the local area. Writing in 1876, Frederick Smeeton Williams observed the building work's dramatic impact in his history of the Midland Railway, recording that the 'passenger station alone swept away a church and seven streets of three thousand houses'. The area demolished for the construction of St Pancras encompassed parts of Somers Town and the whole of Agar Town, which had been developed in the 1840s on land owned by the family of William Agar. By the 1860s this part of London had a reputation for being especially deprived, with poor and insanitary living conditions. The refuse heaps, known ironically as 'La Belle Isle', which stood on the eastern edge of the area, were where refuse from the surrounding neighbourhoods was dumped. Williams's scathing assessment of Agar Town would have left readers with no doubt that the coming of the railway represented the arrival of progress:

> At the broken doors of mutilated houses canaries still sang, and dogs lay basking in the sun, as if to remind one of the vast colonies of bird-fanciers and dog-fanciers who formerly made Agar Town their abode; and from these dwellings came out wretched creatures in rags and dirt, and searched amid the far-extending refuse for the filthy treasure by the aid of which they eked out a miserable livelihood; whilst over the whole neighbourhood the gas-works poured forth their mephitic vapours, and the canal gave forth its rheumatic dampness, extracting in return some of the more poisonous ingredients in the atmosphere, and spreading them upon the surface of the water in a thick scum of various and ominous hues. Such was Agar Town before the Midland Railway came into the midst of it.

King's Cross, London: the Great Dust-Heap, 1837. (Wellcome Library, London)

18 The St Pancras area appeared on Booth's famous map of London poverty

During the late nineteenth century, growing numbers of social investigators and philanthropic campaigners demanded government action to address the extreme poverty afflicting millions living across London. In 1886, Charles Booth, a Liverpool businessman and campaigner for social reform, launched his study *An Inquiry into Life and Labour in London* (1886–1903), which sought to identify the causes of poverty in London and map inequality across the city on a

street-by-street basis. Although his research initially focussed on the East End, Booth soon expanded it to cover the whole of London. His research team's colour-coded maps offer an intricate picture of the dominant income and social-class bracket of inhabitants living in each street. Booth's schema was divided into seven classifications: at the bottom was 'Lowest class. Vicious, semi-criminal', coloured black, and then rising through different shades of purple, blue and red to the 'Upper-middle and upper classes, with 'Wealthy' coloured orange.

In the first edition of Booth's study, published in 1889, the research team used School Board records to categorise each street; however, as the map was updated researchers began to tour London's streets in the company of local policemen and record their impressions in notebooks. Despite a strong commitment to the overarching aim of tackling poverty, their observations often betrayed entrenched class-based assumptions surrounding the morals and character of working-class areas. In reading these comments we see how the solidifying classification of class during the late nineteenth century relied upon a complex mix of material measures entwined with more subjective assumptions.

Overall, Booth's team classified Somers Town as a mixed area, dominated by dark red, lower-middle-class streets, but interspersed with sections of extreme poverty and slum housing. Many among the area's population worked as railway men or mechanics at one of the nearby stations or goods yards.

In 1898, investigator Ernest Aves revisited the area and noted a slight decline in the general tone. Walking around Ossulston Street and the surrounding alleys he observed a largely poor population living in ill-maintained buildings and alongside several brothels and illegal betting houses; however, he also spoke to numerous residents who had lived in the area for a lengthy period of time and were employed in a variety of different roles around Somers Town, including at St Pancras station.

Opposite: North-western sheet of Booth's map, comprising part of Hampstead; Paddington (excepting north-west corner); parts of St George's Hanover Square, Westminster, Strand, Holborn and Islington; the whole of St Giles's and Marylebone, and most of St Pancras. From Charles Booth's *Life and Labour of the People in London*. (Wellcome Library, London)

19   Almost a third of the borough of St Pancras's residents lived in poverty at the turn of the century

Poor housing, overcrowding, and high levels of poverty remained persistent problems across the parish of St Pancras for much of the nineteenth and early twentieth centuries. Housing in the area was in a dilapidated state. The presence of the railways had intensified the problem of overcrowding from the mid-nineteenth century onwards. On the one hand, the construction of station complexes led to the demolition of large amounts of housing, thereby forcing residents into evermore densely packed, sub-divided buildings. On the other, the presence of the railway and of goods yards provided much sought-after work, which drew new arrivals into already crowded areas. In 1902, 30.4 per cent of the borough of St Pancras's residents were living in poverty and 24 per cent in overcrowded rooms. Securing better housing provision and addressing child poverty became prime concerns amongst local residents, campaigners, and philanthropic organisations wanting to improve living conditions in Somers Town from the late-nineteenth century onwards. By the mid 1920s both charities and the London County Council were investing heavily in redeveloping Somers Town's housing stock and demolishing the worst of the area's 'slums'.

20   The Holborn Viaduct was designed by the architect responsible for St Pancras station's roof

London's landscape underwent a profound transformation during the mid-nineteenth century. Designed by Rowland Ordish, who also worked with engineer William Barlow on St Pancras's train shed roof, the Holborn Viaduct was built to ease traffic congestion around the steep Holborn Hill. The viaduct was 1,400ft in length and spanned Farringdon Street to connect Holborn and the City of London. Amongst an array of adverts, Victorian passers-by would have seen the large board advertising the Midland Railway's 'New St Pancras station' and expanded London rail service, which had opened in 1868.

Holborn at the
turn of the century.
(Library of Congress,
LC-DIG-ppmsc-08578)

Sections of the viaduct at Holborn. (Wellcome Library, London)

21 Victorian drinking fountains in and around St Pancras station have survived to the present day

Municipal drinking fountains and horse troughs were a common feature of London street life in the late nineteenth and early twentieth centuries, providing clean drinking water for London's human and animal inhabitants. As understanding of the dangerous effects of London's filthy water supply grew during the 1850s, so an increasing number of voices demanded that more be done to provide a supply of free, safe water. In 1859 the Metropolitan Free Drinking Fountain Association was founded by Samuel Gurney MP, nephew of the prison reformer Elizabeth Fry, with the aim of reducing the reliance of London's poorer inhabitants on badly maintained pumps and river water, which had resulted in frequent cholera outbreaks. The Association drew support from across the

highest echelons of British society and is an example of the prominent role played by philanthropy in improving municipal services in the Victorian period. In 1867 the Association changed its name to the Metropolitan Drinking Fountain and Cattle Trough Association, signalling a growing demand amongst its donors that more be done for the welfare of animals as well as people. By 1870, 140 fountains and 153 troughs had been erected, with many appearing at railway stations. St Pancras station's fountain, recently refurbished and in working order, can be found seen on the eastern wall along Pancras Road; however, the horse trough has been removed.

22 St Christopher's flats were opened by Queen Victoria's granddaughter

St Christopher's flats, which faced onto Bridgewater Street, were opened in November 1931 by Princess Helena Victoria and the Conservative MP, Sir Alfred Beit. Excited crowds gathered along the flats' balconies and in the courtyard to see the opening and their blessing by the Bishop of Truro. They formed part of the new Sidney Estate, which covered 2½ acres of land between (modern-day) Chalton Street, Bridgewater Street, Clarendon Street and Aldenham Street. Six new blocks of flats, each named after saints, were built around a central courtyard, with the development completed in 1938. Reporting on the dynamiting of old housing to clear space for the St Francis block in 1930, *The Times* recorded:

> A spectacular demonstration of slum demolition was given yesterday, when a loud explosion of dynamite told the inhabitants of Somers Town that the Sidney-street area, with its long history of overcrowding, disease, poverty and vermin, was doomed … on the second explosion of the dynamite the flag of St George was broken and the crowd who gathered sang 'New Jerusalem'.

The flats were all furnished with electricity and hot water; *The Times* reminded readers that 'no other working class dwellings in this country are so equipped'. Once completed, St Christopher's flats included a nursery for local children and a roof garden where they could play. Eight years after they opened, the Duke of Kent visited the flats in March 1939, during which he toured the flat of one resident whose son was at home in his railwayman's uniform and worked at St Pancras station.

23 Victorian St Pancras had its own carnival

Patriotic fervour ran high during the spring and summer of 1900 as British troops won a series of victories during the South African War. Despite Britain's numerical and material advantage over the Boer Republics, the war had gone badly in 1899 and early 1900, with a series of humiliating defeats and high casualty rates sapping morale. The relief of Ladysmith, capture of Bloemfontein, and relief of Mafeking in the spring of 1900 sparked jubilant celebrations across British towns and an outpouring of jingoistic support for the empire. The St Pancras area organised its Patriotic Carnival to coincide with and celebrate Queen Victoria's 81st birthday, and was one of many similar events intended to raise money for the *Daily Telegraph* fund for the relief of widows and orphans of soldiers who had fallen in South Africa. Over two days, on 24 and 25 May, the streets around St Pancras station were filled with a parade of carnival floats, injured war veterans and various other celebrations. The press largely endorsed the festivities, praising the bunting and happy mood in the streets, although one reporter wondered whether 'stolid London' was quite ready for the 'thoroughly foreign institution of carnival', while another decried the sight of adults acting like children in the streets. One of the carnival floats sported the crest of the Cape Colony and was populated by a variety of figures in fancy dress celebrating the armed forces and South African colonists. In the centre of the tableau, Britannia could be seen leaning on, rather than sitting astride, a stuffed lion. The carnival raised over £6,000 for the fund; however, hopes that the war would soon be over were premature, with hostilities lasting another two years.

24   The festival-goers at the St Pancras parade in 1930 included four Indian elephants

Planners decided to inject some extra spectacle into the 1930 London Lord Mayor's parade through the inclusion of four Indian elephants. Shortly after their arrival at St Pancras station from India, the elephants were dressed in large ornate howdahs decorated to celebrate the relationship between Britain and India. When they reached St Pancras, they saluted the crowds. With British trade suffering from the debilitating impact of the Great Depression, the parade was seen to offer an ideal opportunity to encourage Londoners to support economic recovery by buying empire goods. In the event, however, the day descended into chaos as two of the elephants, labelled 'Imports' and 'Exports', charged into the crowd midway along the Embankment. The press speculated that the animals had been scared by a group of King's College students letting off fireworks, shouting, and waving a red plaster-of-Paris lion in the air. One of the elephants seized the lion, while another shook its howdah into the crowd. Amidst the panic around thirty people were injured in the melee, although none by the elephants. In the aftermath, the Principal of King's College, Dr W.R. Halliday, denied that any blame could be attributed to his students' 'ragging' of the elephants, suggesting instead that the animals 'were bored by the whole proceeding and seeing a wide opening at the entrance to the college tried to get through away from the crowd'!

25   Sights in Edwardian St Pancras included Suffragette Rallies

On the afternoon of 7 November 1908, a rally organised by Flora Drummond, a leading figure in the Women's Social and Political Union, marched from Kingsway to Holloway Prison in support of female suffrage. It passed by St Pancras station. The 500-strong rally marked a show of support for fellow Suffragettes imprisoned in Holloway, including Emmeline and Christabel Pankhurst, who were then being held in solitary confinement. Nicknamed 'The General', Flora Drummond had only been released from Holloway four days earlier, after the Liberal Home Secretary, Herbert Gladstone, signed an order of release

A WSPU meeting in around 1906: Flora Drummond (*left*) can here be seen with Christabel and Emmeline Pankhurst, Annie Kenney, and Charlotte Despard. (LSE, 7JCC/O/02/109)

from her three-month sentence for 'incitement to rush the House of Commons' when it was discovered she was pregnant. The press reported that as they marched the women 'lustily sang the Women's Marseillaise' accompanied by a brass band. Several marchers were dressed in imitation prison clothes, comprising a green blouse and skirt, with prisoner's number on the breast, and a white cap. By the time they reached Holloway Prison the crowd had swelled to several thousand strong and was addressed by Flora Drummond and Sylvia Pankhurst. Groups of men were also prominent in the crowd, some of whom cheered their support while others engaged in mocking chants. Speaking afterwards, Sylvia Pankhurst voiced her pleasure at the rally's success, declaring, 'It is one of the best things we have done.'

26   Suffragettes picketed St Pancras's MP

The January 1910 general election campaign was marked by widespread demonstrations by female suffrage campaigners opposed to the Liberal government and demanding votes for women. The constituency of South St Pancras saw significant resistance as 'suffragette hit squads' targeted the Liberal MP, Philip Whitwell Wilson, picketing political meetings and polling stations. The South St Pancras operation was organised by the artist Hilda Dallas from the committee rooms at 7 St Andrews Mansions, Newman Street. The suffrage movement had deep roots in north London, with prominent campaigners living across St Pancras from the mid-nineteenth century. Although the Liberal government had proposed a Suffrage Bill in 1909, which would have enfranchised some women, it was delayed by the controversy surrounding the People's Budget and then dropped when the General Election was called for January 1910. At the same time, Henry Herbert Asquith's Liberal government adopted an increasingly repressive and draconian response towards suffrage campaigners, with mounting numbers imprisoned for public order offenses. The Liberals saw their majority slashed in the January election, including losing the seat of South St Pancras to the Conservative and Unionist candidate. Even though a new Conciliation Bill aimed at granting the vote to some women was passed in June 1910, this too was abandoned after a fresh election was held in November 1910. Women in Britain had to wait until 1918 for limited female suffrage, when those over 30 or householders over 21 gained the vote through the 1918 Representation of the People Act, and until 1928 for women over the age of 21 to receive the vote on the same terms as men.

27 When women were granted the vote, many UCH nurses cast their first ballot in St Pancras

During the 1935 General Election, many groups of young nurses, from nearby University College Hospital (UCH), were directed towards a St Pancras polling station. UCH was founded in 1834 as a teaching hospital to educate medical students from University College London, after governors of the nearby Middlesex Hospital had refused to allow students access to their wards. During the 1860s, it began helping with the training nurses sent to the hospital by the All Saints Sisters of the Poor, and by 1919 was running professional qualification courses for nursing. Following the Representation of the People Act of 1928, which enfranchised all women over the age of 21, it is likely that this would have been the first time these young women had voted. The 1935 election resulted in the Conservative Party gaining a majority of seats (including those in St Pancras), despite the Labour Party gaining its greatest vote share up until that point. This was the last election before the end of the Second World War.

28   One of the first female MPs represented Holborn and St Pancras South

Labour Party parliamentary candidate Lena Jeger spoke to St Pancras railway workers during the 1953 Holborn and St Pancras South by-election. Already popular for her work as a London County Councillor, Lena Jeger was selected by the constituency party to contest the election following the death of the incumbent MP and her husband, Dr Santo Jeger. The recent nationalisation of the railways and large number of railway workers living in the constituency made this an important group to win over in what was a marginal seat. In its coverage of the campaign, *The Guardian* described a diverse community, where different classes lived 'cheek by jowl'. Lena Jeger's campaign focused on key social problems faced by many working-class constituents in post-war 'austerity Britain', including efforts to combat homelessness and poverty, and to provide better financial support to widows. Following a series of high-profile campaign visits from leading figures in the party, she secured victory by over 1,900 votes, making her only the twenty-first female MP to enter parliament. She held the seat until the 1959 election, when she narrowly lost to the Conservative candidate, Geoffrey Johnson Smith, and subsequently became Chair of the Labour Party. In 1979, Lena Jeger was created a life peer as Baroness Jeger of St Pancras.

29   The Great Depression affected the St Pancras area

In 1932, in midst of the Great Depression, such a large queue formed in response to a job opportunity at the Regent Theatre on the Euston Road that *The Daily Herald* sent reporters to investigate it. They found a long queue snaking its way along the road. Police were present to maintain order, with men and women separated into different queues. Unemployment stood at just over 1.7 million at the start of 1932 and would rise to almost 3 million by its conclusion. Large numbers were forced to compete for poorly-paid and insecure jobs, with any opportunity for work often attracting lines of applicants similar to those encountered by the reporters.

30   St Pancras station witnessed the National Hunger March of 27 October 1932

The final stage of the National Hunger March passed St Pancras station en route to its conclusion in Hyde Park. By late 1932 unemployment in Britain stood at 2,750,000, around 15 per cent of the workforce. Over the preceding months, there had been a growing number of confrontations across the country between police and protesters demanding the government do more to help the out of work. The National Hunger March was organised by the National Unemployed Workers Movement and involved around 3,000 marchers from across the country converging in London on 27 October 1932. In pouring rain the marchers arrived in Hyde Park, where they were greeted by crowds of around 100,000, but also 70,000 police. Violent clashes ensued, with mounted police charging the crowd in several places and protesters throwing iron railings and bricks. Although the economy slowly started to recover after 1932, unemployment remained high and welfare support limited. As the decade progressed, several further marches took place as unemployed workers protested the government's inaction in addressing unemployment and voiced their opposition to the widely hated Welfare Means Test.

31   There was a May Day riot in Ossulston Street

Tempers flared at the 1958 annual May Day rally organised by the St Pancras and Holborn Trades Council in Ossulston Street. The summer of 1958 would be characterised by a series of violent encounters across the country, culminating in the Notting Hill race riots, as far-right groups clashed with new migrant communities and left-wing counter-protesters. Tensions boiled over in the St Pancras area on 5 May: at around 7 a.m. Labour-supporting council activists hoisted the Red Flag over St Pancras Town Hall, whilst a loudspeaker van spent the morning touring the area promoting the day's events, which had been approved by the local authorities. However, the fascist British Union and groups of students clad in Union Jacks attempted to disrupt the May Day celebrations and stage a counter-demonstration also in Ossulston Street. Fearing violent clashes, the police ordered the abandonment of the May Day rally. Angered that this appeared to favour their opponents, the May Day campaigners refused to move, with *The Times* reporting that Labour Councillor John Lawrence had 'just warmed up to an attack on the Government and Mr Brooke, the Minister of Housing and Local Government, in particular' when he was dragged from the stage by a number of officers. More police, including some on horseback, emerged from within the Somers Town Goods Yard and tried forcibly to disperse the gathering. When the crowd responded with shouts of 'fascists' and sang 'The Red Flag', police officers began making arrests. Skirmishes continued throughout the afternoon, with ten people, seven men and three women, arrested and charged with public order offenses.

32 The Notting Hill Carnival began in St Pancras Town Hall

In January 1959 the first Caribbean Carnival, forerunner of the Notting Hill Carnival, took place at St Pancras Town Hall. During the summer of 1958 violent race riots swept Notting Hill as ongoing racial tensions between the area's Caribbean and white communities erupted into sustained street violence. The Caribbean community in Notting Hill had grown steadily during the 1950s as the numbers of West Indian migrants coming to Britain rose after 1945. As racial friction in the area mounted, right-wing groups and politicians, including Oswald Moseley, looked to capitalise by making inflammatory speeches that demanded Britain be kept white. Racially motivated attacks increased during the summer of 1958, until on the night of 30 August a group of around 500, mainly young white men, took to the streets attacking houses and West Indian residents. The violence continued nightly until 5 September and resulted in over 140 arrests.

News coverage of the riots and aftermath tended to be heavily racialised in tone and highly critical of the effects of non-white immigration. Motivated by a desire to raise community morale and resist racial discrimination, community leaders strove for new ways to celebrate Caribbean culture. Key among them was the writer and activist Claudia Jones, who organised the first Notting Hill Carnival in January 1959 to assert a sense of 'pride in being West Indian'. Due to the cold weather, it was held indoors at St Pancras Town Hall, which stands opposite the station, and directed by the singer and performer

Edric Connor. Performances included sets by the Boscoe Holder Dance Troupe and singer Cleo Laine, as well as a contest for Carnival Queen. The carnival continued to be held each January until Jones's death in December 1964, after which it moved to its current site in Notting Hill, where it continues to draw over 1 million participants every August on the anniversary of the riots.

33   A St Pancras headliner was once banned from the UK by MI5

International music star Paul Robeson played at St Pancras Town Hall for the anniversary concert for the *West Indian Gazette* in September 1960, generating much excitement in the press and amongst the public. Robeson had been due to appear in concert at the same venue in 1957;

however, after the US government withdrew his passport on the grounds that his right to travel contravened the national interest, MI5 recommended that he be banned from entering the UK. This decision spurred the emergence of the 'Let Robeson Sing' campaign, where he sang for audiences in England and Wales through the transatlantic telephone cable. Such was his popularity that the 1,000 tickets for his 1957 telephone concert at St Pancras Town Hall sold out within an hour.

Paul Robeson. (Library of Congress, LC-USF34-013362-C)

Paul Leroy Robeson (9 April 1898–23 January 1976) was an American singer, actor and political activist of global renown. Having first gained fame as a college football player, he went onto star in a series of Hollywood films, theatre productions, and recorded over 276 songs during his lifetime. Nevertheless, his opposition towards the Spanish Civil War and fascism, and his advocacy for the civil rights and anti-colonial movements, resulted in him being branded a radical communist, and placed on the Hollywood blacklist during the McCarthy era. In June 1958, the Supreme Court ruled that it was unconstitutional to deny a US passport on political grounds and Robeson was able to begin touring again. He spent two years in the UK, including the anniversary concert at St Pancras Town Hall, during which he commemorated the cultural significance and political achievements of the 1957 show.

34 There was a riot in St Pancras Town Hall on Armistice Day 1961

Racial tension and violence continued to simmer around the St Pancras area throughout the late 1950s and 1960s. A fight broke out at a meeting held at St Pancras Town Hall on Armistice Day 1961, which had been organised in opposition to the government's new immigration restrictions. Members of the League of Empire Loyalists and the fascist Union Movement, mainly comprising young white men, stormed the meeting and seized the stage shouting 'Keep Britain white' and overturning tables. Fights broke out as members of the audience clashed with the protestors, and the evening descended into a violent brawl.

35   The Prime Minister once gave a speech in the constituency from the back of a lorry

On 30 September 1964, Prime Minister Alec Douglas Home made a campaign appearance in St Pancras – a little over a fortnight before the general election – addressing the gathered crowd from the back of a lorry driven between campaign stops. The constituency of Holborn and St Pancras South was held by the Conservative Party, but only by a narrow margin, and the Prime Minister was met by a crowd of protesters carrying banners decrying the Polaris nuclear programme. As he spoke their jeers and heckles became so loud that he was forced to cut his speech short. One of these 'long-haired Wandsworth rowdies', as *The Guardian* described the agitators, was seen wielding a half brick, but was prevented from throwing anything at the prime minister as he stood on the Union Jack-bedecked platform. The constituency of Holborn and St Pancras South had a diverse population – encompassing Holborn and the southern half of the metropolitan borough of St Pancras, around Bloomsbury, Euston, King's Cross, and Somers Town. The area had recently seen high immigration from the Commonwealth; around 1,500 Greek Cypriots had settled in the area in the preceding decade, and the local Labour Party courted their votes. But there were also other demographic changes, as rising prices forced residents from central London; in 1964, Holborn and St Pancras South had over 10,000 voters fewer than in 1950, in no small part driven out by market forces. At the election, the marginal seat was won by Lena Jeger, for the Labour Party, and remained in the party's hands until the constituency was merged with St Pancras North in 1983.

36   Mothers once picketed St Pancras Town Hall

On 25 May 1939, a few months before the outbreak of the Second World War, a group of mothers and children picketed St Pancras Town Hall demanding free milk provision for mothers and babies. The protests gained momentum early in 1939 after the council introduced new regulations making it more difficult for poorer mothers to access free or subsidised milk. In February, a series of 'pram protest marches' took place through the streets of the borough to collect signatures for a petition, which included the names of over eighty local doctors, whilst the protest in May involved a sit-in on the steps of the town hall. Under the headline 'Councils Save at Babies' Expense' *The Daily Herald* reported that councilmen had had to step over mothers and children, who were singing 'We want milk' to the tune of 'The Lambeth Walk'. During the ensuing debate, mothers cheered from the gallery as female councillors demanded action. When the vote was lost uproar ensued, with one mother, carrying her baby, physically ejected from the council chamber.

The issue revealed the tensions at the heart of local life in the 1930s, and, in particular, the divisions between wealthier and poorer residents of St Pancras borough. Anger had mounted after the council indulged the expense of building a new town hall, completed in 1937, but proved unwilling to provide for the welfare of the borough's poorest residents. One outraged Labour councillor even accused a Tory counterpart of proclaiming 'that if mothers did not feed their children gin they would have more to spend on milk'. Throughout the nineteenth and twentieth centuries, local residents were consistently vocal in demanding improved housing and health provision from local authorities. While these campaigns were frequently undertaken in collaboration with philanthropic organisations, the impetus for change often came from within the local community. Although St Pancras' residents had to wait until after the war, the 1946 School Milk Act provided free milk to all children under the age of 18.

37   David Bailey and Catherine Deneuve married at St Pancras Town Hall

In the summer of 1965, St Pancras Town Hall played host to the year's hottest celebrity wedding. At St Pancras Registry Office on 18 August 1965, the marriage of glamourous British fashion photographer David Bailey and his bride, the celebrated French actress, Catherine Deneuve, exuded the spirit of 1960s Swinging London. The celebrity couple met a few months earlier during the filming of Roman Polanski's *Repulsion*, before becoming better acquainted when Bailey photographed her for *Playboy* magazine. The superstar wedding garnered extensive press coverage and public attention: Mick Jagger acted as best man, the groom wore jeans and no tie for the occasion, while the bride smoked throughout the ceremony, much to the priest's dismay. Bailey and Deneuve stayed together for three years, before divorcing in 1972; Bailey described his marriage being 'like trying to manage a Maserati when you're used to a Ford', while Deneuve pithily observed that 'marriage is obsolete and a trap'.

38   There was briefly an RAF base in a St Pancras railway yard

On 11 May 1969, the *Daily Mail* Transatlantic Air Race saw Royal Navy and Royal Air Force Phantoms racing in a round trip from the Empire State Building in New York to the Post Office Tower (now the BT Tower) in London. The GR1 Harrier Jet Engine was chosen by the Royal Air Force because of its ability to land without a runway using a 'hovering' method – necessary when landing in central London. Although initially rejected due to the large mounds of coal that filled it,

St Pancras's railway yard ultimately was used as a landing site during the race, and was briefly renamed 'RAF St Pancras'. Squadron leader Tom Lecky-Thompson stated it took only six minutes to get from the Tower to lifting off at St Pancras railway yard, which helped him win in a time of six hours, eleven minutes. The use of the railway yard not only showcased the Harrier Jet's technological sophistication but also provided a fitting backdrop that captured the imagination of the media and spectators alike.

39 The Beatles did a photoshoot at St Pancras Old Church garden

The Beatles were photographed in a playful pose around the fountain in St Pancras Old Church garden on 28 July 1969. Taking a break from recording their White Album, the band spent the day travelling around various London sites with photographers Stephen Goldblatt and Don McCullin.

Tucked just behind St Pancras station, the church is believed to be one of the oldest sites of Christian worship in Britain. The gardens have a similarly rich history, and include a memorial sundial dedicated to philanthropist Baroness Burdett-Coutts, who was responsible for converting the gardens to public use. The fountain was made for the senior churchwarden of St Pancras, William Thornton, as a drinking fountain for the poor of the parish, and manufactured by Andrew Handyside and Co. of Derbyshire in 1877. Since 1998 it has been listed as a Grade II English Heritage item in 1998. Large crowds congregated to see the Beatles messing around during their impromptu visit. Wearing brightly coloured suits, they posed amongst the garden's flower beds and paused to have their photos taken with local fans.

40   Mr Universe was once held at St Pancras Assembly Rooms

In September 1971, contestants at the 19th National Amateur Body Builder Association (NABBA) Mr Universe competition lined up in the Assembly Rooms in St Pancras Town Hall. Despite the incongruity of the surroundings, the contest has remained shrouded in controversy. A split within the bodybuilding governing body meant that Arnold Schwarzenegger, the reigning champion, did not compete at St Pancras, choosing instead to appear as the only competitor at a rival competition in Paris the following week, where he was crowned Mr Olympia. In London, Bill Pearl was crowned Mr Universe over Sergio Oliva, despite many observers believing the latter had far larger and superior muscles. Schwarzenegger subsequently recalled:

> If there was ever one contest I wanted to enter it was the 1971 NABBA Pro Mr. Universe in London because Sergio Oliva and Bill Pearl had entered ... Sergio was big and Bill was big and cut, but I was even bigger and more cut. I consider 1971 to be my best ever year as I was totally ripped at 246 pounds. And I just felt that I would go to London and destroy those guys.

41   The space today occupied by the British Library was intended for housing

With pressure on local housing mounting during the early 1970s, Somers Town residents lobbied Camden Council to build new homes on disused railway land around St Pancras station. The Somers Town Action Group, made up of representatives from local tenants' organisations, took a leading role in the campaign, drawing up a plan that outlined the residents' proposals for redevelopment. The forcefully worded report highlighted the enduring sense of neglect felt amongst the Somers Town community, drawing specific attention to the poor conditions that came from living in a heavily built-up area in close proximity to the railway. The Group demanded more and better housing for local families and green spaces designed to be used by elderly people and young children. The Camden residents' newsletter triumphantly reported the land's acquisition and the further involvement of tenants in planning and building homes. Such celebration proved to be premature, however, as the construction of housing was delayed, and ultimately cancelled. Instead, the decision was taken in 1975 that the site on which the Somers Town Goods Yard stood would be filled by the new British Library building.

42   There has been a Somers Town Festival for more than twenty years

For the last twenty years, the Somers Town Festival of Cultures has taken place each summer in celebration of the area's diversity and pride in its local identity. Although Somers Town held an annual festival in the 1960s and '70s, the area struggled during the 1980s as youth unemployment soared, far-right groups gained a foothold, and tensions and violence escalated between different ethnic communities. Organised by local activists Steve Denholm and Alan Patterson, the Festival of Cultures started in 1996 in a neighbourhood community centre as a unifying challenge to these local divisions. Initial success saw the event quickly grow and move to Chalton Street market, where in 2000 it celebrated the 75th anniversary of the St Pancras Housing Trust. Its success has helped launch Somers Town Art [START], which supports local artists, musicians, and community projects. Asked about the crucial element of a good community festival in a 2016 interview, Steve Denholm observed, 'Sunshine and the music. Most important – the stalls bring together people who want to sell food, share information, health and welfare.'

Today the festival draws thousands each July to enjoy a range of stalls, a funfair, and performances that celebrate Somers Town's rich mix of communities. Describing the 2016 Festival, START wrote:

> We had Bengali music, retro punk, Josie's young dance group, surreal performance art, the new line up of the Somers Town Blues Band, free massages from Women and Health, vintage make up from Working men's college, Pearly Queens, youth performance 'The Plan' from Small green shoots, Somers Town Futures, acupuncture, drawing, bubbles, fresh juice stalls, dancing from Josie's new group, the British Library, science from The Francis Crick, Chilean empanadas, African Drumming, a History stall, a reinvented Big Brother celeb Becki debut on stage, Mimi's anti HS2 singalong, and a very British singalong with Pearly Queens.
>
> But the bubble man trumped all as our favourite attraction! – simple pleasures are best!

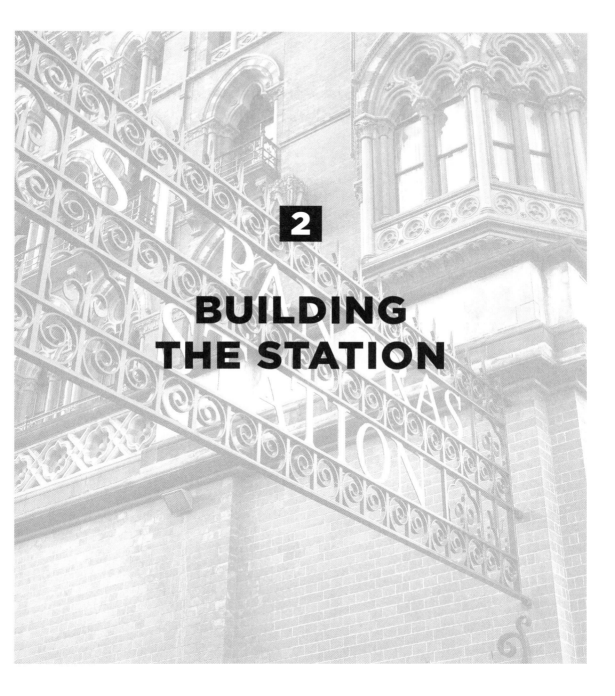

2

BUILDING
THE STATION

43 32,000 Londoners were displaced by the building of the Midland Railway

The path of the Midland Railway line cut across many houses, gardens, the St Pancras burial ground, and roads in Agar and Somers Towns. The Midland Railway began purchasing land and leases in the area from 1860, and subsequently allowed many houses to fall into disrepair, before a parliamentary bill of 1864 gave the Company right of compulsory purchase in order to construct the line and sidings through Somers Town. When construction began in 1866 the whole of Agar Town disappeared in under two months. Ultimately, around 4,000 houses were demolished and 32,000 people displaced and forced to find new accommodation in the surrounding areas. Some moved north into Kilburn but many remained around Somers Town living in ever more cramped circumstances. As historian Steven Denford observes, it seems more than coincidence that applications to the St Pancras workhouse rose significantly in 1866. Today, the only reminder of Agar Town's existence is Agar Grove, a street that runs along the edge of where the town once stood.

44 Midland Railway built a special viaduct to take trains over the graves at St Pancras Old Church

Laborers employed by the Waring Company for the Midland Railway Company constructed a tunnel to connect the overland railway to the underground Metropolitan Line, which had opened in 1863. The tunnel remains in use today as part of the Thameslink system. Each man earned 4s 6d a day, whilst young boys were paid a shilling less. During the peak of railway building in the mid-nineteenth century there were over 250,000 navvies at work on lines across Britain.

The graves at St Pancras Old Church. Etching by G. Cooke, 1827. (Wellcome Library, London)

  The final stages of construction of St Pancras's train shed and the Midland Railway extension that connected Bedford to London began in 1867 and 1868. By early 1868 the extension of the Midland Railway line had almost reached the Euston Road. The contract to construct the final section of track from just north of the Regent's Canal to the terminus, totalling just 1,320 yards, had been given to the firm Waring Brothers and cost £319,000 to complete. As the Midland Railway extension approached the new station it had to cross the St Pancras Old Church burial ground. Government legislation stipulated that the construction works should create as little disturbance as possible to the graves, requiring an iron viaduct to be constructed to carry the main line over most of the cemetery. A small locomotive was used to bring equipment and workers onto the site. Another new brick and iron bridge carried St Pancras Road over the railway line, which ran beneath. Pulleys and chains were used to manouevre the thick struts and bricks into place, whilst a wooden bridge carried the temporary rail track used to transport men and equipment during the construction.

45   The Midland Railway was also diverted to avoid the Fleet River

One thing the railway was not allowed to cut across was the Fleet River. Since its enclosure in 1825, the Fleet River had served as one of London's principal sewers and ran directly across the path of the new railway, emptying into the Thames at Blackfriars. Outbreaks of cholera ravaged Somers Town and Agar Town in the mid 1860s, with the Metropolitan Board of Works demanding that the line not disrupt the sewer for fear of further epidemic. Subsequently, the Fleet was enclosed in a massive iron pipe, in which it continues to run down the western side of Pancras Road.

The mouth of the Fleet in 1725; the river is now entirely covered over. (Wellcome Library, London)

46   St Pancras station was built using horse-drawn carts

Even as workmen made use of new steam-powered engines, cranes, and pumps to move heavy material, more traditional technologies remained essential during the construction operation. Horse-drawn carts were used to deliver the coal required to power the machinery. A mobile crane mounted in a wooden shed moved materials into place during the construction of the brick cellars. The crane travelled on temporary tracks and was used to lift heavy materials whilst workmen constructed the cellar's walls. In order to avoid creating a steep gradient just outside the station, the rail line crossed over the Regent's Canal rather than going under it. This meant that St Pancras' platforms stood 17ft above the level of the Euston Road. Rather than fill the space beneath the platforms with earth, the platform level, was, and remains, supported by 15ft-high iron columns. This represented a calculated architectural departure from a system of brick piers and arches, and created much more space for storage.

47   St Pancras station's roof contains 2.5 acres of glass

With the railway extension fast approaching in autumn 1867, the station's iron roof started to be erected. Before each section of ironwork could be put in place a giant latticed wooden scaffolding had to be constructed to allow builders to raise the 105ft arch. The scaffold alone was 40ft wide, contained 25,000cu.ft of timber, and weighed 480 tons.
    According to Williams:

Under ordinary circumstances, an erection of this kind would consist of two side walls with a roof resting upon them, but in this instance it may be described as all roof. The girders of the walls and roof spring directly from the undermost foundation, and the iron floor of the station takes the place of ties which hold the whole together. These roof girders, too, are of remarkable construction, resembling in their appearance a lobster's claw, from which the shorter nipper has been broken off; and instead of being set, so to speak, horizontally, they are fixed vertically in pairs, the two-pointed extremities meeting, and forming a Gothic arch overhead.

The Illustrated London News proclaimed that:

Their magnitude far exceeds anything else of this kind. Half Somers Town was demolished to make room for the new station and hotel, which occupy, including the station yard, about ten acres ... It is really wonderful to see the manner in which this huge fabric is put together, piece by piece, rising in the boldest curves from the massive iron 'springers' on each side, and meeting at the ridge of the roof.

During the construction of the roof, a rail-mounted steam-powered winch was used to hoist the steel cables and ironwork up from ground level. Workmen fed cable into the winch to be hauled up the scaffolding. Construction of the roof was undertaken by the Butterley Iron Company, which also produced all of the iron work. Labourers were paid *5s 2½d* a day, Strikers *5s 6d*, while smiths, fitters and rivetters all earned *8s* or over a day. Boys employed on the site were paid at the rate of *4s 2d* a day.

Early progress on the roof proved slow, with Barlow submitting a formal complaint to the Butterley Company in November 1867. By March the following year, however, the work was quickening. An additional scaffold had been constructed allowing for three or four

The station at the turn of the century. (Publishers Collection)

of the iron ribs to be put in place each month. During construction, what would become the station platform provided a bay on which a travelling stage was constructed. Comprised of three distinct sections – a middle, and two sides – when one bay was completed – bolted together and stayed – the staging moved forwards: first, one side of it, then the other side, and finally the middle. Then the construction of the framing for the next main rib began. The last rib was fitted in September 1868, and despite much of the interior not being finished the station welcomed its first arrival on 1 October 1868.

Describing the monumental proportions of the train shed in his 1878 volume of *Old and New London*, Edward Walford wrote:

[The roof] is 100 feet high, 700 feet in length, and its width about 240 feet. The span of the roof covers four platforms, eleven lines of rails, and a cab-stand twenty-five feet wide; altogether the station occupies a site of nearly ten acres. There are twenty-five principal ribs in the roof, and the weight of each is about fifty tons. The very scaffolding, by the help of which the roof was raised into its position, contained eight miles of massive timber, 1,000 tons in weight, besides about 25,000 cubic feet of wood, and eighty tons of ironwork. No other roof of so vast a span has been attempted. It is double the width of the Agricultural Hall at Islington, and ten yards wider than the two arches of the neighbouring terminus of the Great Northern Railway, which, when first built, were considered a triumph of engineering skill. Some idea may be formed of the vast expanse of the roof of the Midland Terminus when we state that it contains no less than two acres and a half of glass. The gigantic main ribs cost a thousand pounds apiece. These and the other interior portions of the framework are painted a sky-blue, and by this means the roof is made to look particularly light and airy.

48   The station is made with 60 million bricks

The interior of the station was planned with great care. St Pancras represented an opportunity for the Midland Railway to celebrate the Company's regional roots by showcasing the finest examples of Midlands' industry, manufacturing, and craftsmanship. The distinctive red bricks were made by Edward Gripper of Nottingham using his special patented method; the Mansfield, Ketton and Ancaster stone used in the archways and dressings were all quarried in the Midlands; while Butterley's was a Derby firm, the same city in which the Midland Railway had its headquarters.

When describing the interior of the station to its readers in the month of its opening, *The London Journal* observed 'the quiet and pleasing' effect of the 60 million bricks and 80,000cu.ft of dressed stone that made up the station:

The ironwork is coloured chocolate, and the boarding French gray ...
The platforms have edges of dressed stone, and are floored with red deal
planks, dressed, close-jointed, and tongued with hoops iron ... There are
four platforms and a carriage road; and eleven lines of rails, with room for
two more, that are intentionally left out for the present for convenience in
carting to and from the station. Excepting one along the side of the wall,
the platforms are available at both edges. A very handsome tessellated
frieze, about 2 feet deep, is being inland with Minton's coloured tiles.
The moulding above the frieze will be surmounted by an iron casting
of floral design, the leaves to curve inwards from the cornice. The face
principal at the entrance to the station is a fine piece of ironwork, and
presents a commanding appearance, the effect being much enhanced
by the cresting round the end of the roof, with pinnacle at the apex. The
side walls are being finished by a projecting base of best Nottingham red
bricks, returned round the feet of the principals with Staffordshire blue
bricks and capped by a massive moulding of red Mansfield stone.

49   St Pancras station's cellars cover more than 4.5 acres

Describing the construction process for the cellars in 1876, the chronicler of the Midland Railway, Frederick Smeeton Williams, recorded:

[W]e must now go down into the foundations and see how the work of construction is being carried on. In what seems to be the confusion of earthworks worse confounded, the men are laying vast quantities of concrete one-and-twenty feet down in the London clay, and fifty-four feet below the surface of the ground; on these they will build massive brick piers; the piers will carry the columns that support the floor, and each brick pier will have to stand a pressure of five-and-fifty tons Gradually order appears. The work of 100 steam lifts, 1,000 horses, and 6,000 men, tell their tale. The colossal brick walls and arches which form the underground tunnels are built deep down in the cuttings prepared to receive them; 720 cast-iron columns, each thirteen inches in diameter, are set with stone bases on the piers; across the station are forty-nine main wrought iron girders; fifteen similar ones are placed longitudinally; 2,000 intermediate girders and innumerable 'buckle' plates are riveted together; and thus arise four acres and a half of what will serve at once as the roof of the cellars and the floor of the future passenger station. Its strength is everywhere sufficient to carry the enormous weight of locomotives. The cost of the ironwork was £3 a square yard.

50 St Pancras station's undercroft was modelled on the beer warehouses of Burton-on-Trent

Even though the intricate neo-gothic frontage of George Gilbert Scott's Midland Hotel has tended to dominate in many depictions of St Pancras, the vast iron and brick train shed constituted no less a feat of engineering. Designed by engineer William Barlow in 1866, upon completion the latticed iron roof would span 73.15 metres to create the largest single enclosed space in the world. Butterley Ironwork Company of Derby gained the contract to construct the roof, with the same ironwork installed in the 1860s still in place today.

The space beneath the station floor, meanwhile, now filled with shops and the Eurostar Terminal, was used for storing barrels of Burton beer. St Pancras's foundations were quite literally shaped around a barrel of beer. The station undercroft, as well as the Pancras good shed north of the canal, provided storage space for the main commodity arriving from the Midlands, Burton beer. The spacing of the columns at just over 14ft apart was calculated to fit multiples of the standard cask and modelled to match the dimensions of the beer warehouses of Burton upon Trent. As Barlow put it: 'the length of a beer barrel became the unit of measure upon which all the arrangements of this floor were based'. Brewing was the staple industry of Burton, or 'Beer City' as it was popularly known, where the local water reputedly contained the perfect mineral content to make light beers. Several of Britain's largest breweries were based there and relied upon the Midland Railway to transport barrels and bottles to London. Many breweries were directly connected to the railway and by the late nineteenth century produced a trainload of beer a day. One of the largest, Bass, developed a particularly close relationship with the Midland Railway. In the late 1880s, Bass employed over 2,500 men and each year brewed the equivalent of 70,000 acres of barley and

4,000 acres of hops. The Company's London Ale Stores were situated just behind the station in 'a noble building, bounded on one side by the King's Road, on another by the Regent's Canal, and on the other by the Midland Railway Company's wharf, its shape being nearly triangular', which was leased from the Midland Railway. Built over three floors and capable of holding 160,000 barrels, the stores covered a total area of 5 acres and were directly connected to the railway, and Regent's Canal by a wharf. Bass employed 150 men on the site and incorporated a series of hydraulic lifts to move barrels between floors.

In total, the cost of constructing the whole station, not including the hotel, amounted to £435,882 12s 6d. Alfred Barnard's four-volume account of Britain's breweries provides an illuminating sketch of Burton brewer's Thomas Salt & Co.'s gaslit beer stores in the St Pancras undercroft:

> We found ourselves in the largest of the stores, stretching out right and left from the doorway as far as the eye could reach. At the extreme corner is the stock sample room, where a cask of every gyle is kept for examination, and where the temperature is always maintained at 52 degrees Fahr. Here customers come to sample the beer before they purchase it, and are thus able to ascertain its condition, strength and quality. These extensive stores, covering nearly half an acre, are divided by a double line of railway, in the centre of which is a turn-table for two wagons. This railway is in direct communication with the high level service, and a train with beer arrives from Burton daily.
>
> The first division, which is called No. 1 store, and will hold 20,000 barrels, is entered from the street by two spacious and lofty arches, which are used for loading out the beer. It measures 350 feet by 100 feet, the height is 16 feet, and the arches above are supported by no less than 126 massive iron columns. The premises, which are well ventilated, are paved with brick and drained by a thorough system of double trap drains. Walking to the north end of the No. 1 store we came to a large

vaulted apartment, used as a bottling store by Messrs. Moody & Co., who bottle Messrs. Salt's ales in London, for the home and export trade. It is well arranged for the purpose, being fitted up with all the usual bottling appliances and machines. Extending in front of it there is a large space covered with casks of ale reserved for Messrs. Moody's use ... Leaving the bottling stores behind us, we crossed the railway track, and entered the second division referred to. At the entrance, numbers of workmen were busy unloading the trucks and rolling the casks of ale into the stores, whilst others were taking the numbers and re-marking the casks. This store is scarcely as large as the other, and has an exit onto the opposite side into the Midland Road, so it will be seen that the two places take up the whole width of St Pancras station. A short distance higher up the road, under some more arches of the railway, are the stables and dray sheds of the firm, where fifteen horses are stabled and seven vehicles housed. As most of the carting is done by contract, especially in distant parts of London, these horses are used principally for delivering ale in the immediate locality. Returning to the office we refreshed ourselves with a glass of Messrs Salt's best pale ale, and once more set out on our travels.

51   The Grand Hotel took seven years to build

First opened to guests unfinished in 1873, George Gilbert Scott's Midland Grand Hotel projected the wealth and confidence of the Midland Railway Company as it established itself in London. Scott's elaborate Neo-Gothic exterior was matched by magnificent interior decoration that promised guests 'every convenience and luxury', including even ten pianos of varying sizes, all made from the finest walnut, placed around the public sitting rooms. Describing the station and hotel in *Belgravia: a London Magazine* in 1875, the journalist, Henry Lake, wrote:

The Midland Grand Hotel, is, however, the chief and most interesting feature of the immense pile. From first to last it will, when finished, about eighteen months from this time, have occupied seven years in its erection. The visitors' rooms number nearly 600, and are fitted with a luxurious taste heretofore unknown in this country. The hotel has been built from the designs of Sir Gilbert George Scott, R.A., and the contactors were Messrs Jackson and Shaw. The whole interior is perfect. Elevated considerably from the level of the road, there is neither noise nor dust of traffic. By special arrangements of the architect not a sound

of the adjacent railway is heard. Perfect noiselessness even to a footfall is secured by the solidity of the walls and the thickness of the carpets in the rooms and corridors. Every appliance that luxury can conceive is here to be found. The *salle à manger*, though only of a temporary character, and to be superseded by the great hall not yet finished, is fitted in the best taste. But for the carpet on the floor you could imagine yourself in the finest hotel on the Continent, but even there you would be puzzled to find any room so luxurious. The whole of the internal decoration and furnishing were instrusted to Messrs Gillow and Son, and certainly these celebrated decorators will gather many an applauding criticism for the unique character of their work ... The fabric of this hotel will cost £350,000, and the decorations and furniture £150,000 more. But when finished it will be the most magnificent in the world, and will probably decide the point of arrival for many travellers from the North. There is an immense comfort in finding yourself with only a few feet of platform between you and your hotel when you arrive, and a sense of security on departure when a servant of the hotel obtains your ticket and your seats, and informs you of the last moment before departure. Americans especially, who are used to first-class establishments in their country, have already marked it for their own; and many of them who have arrived from Liverpool, Manchester, and Leeds declare that 'there is no hotel on this planet which equals the Grand Hotel, St Pancras.'

Opposite: The Midland Grand.

52 The frontage of the Midland Grand took a further three years to complete

Even after the station had opened, building work continued in earnest. Construction of the Midland Grand, which would form the station's elaborate frontage on Euston Road, did not start until 1867 and was only finally completed in 1877. Commenting on the ongoing works *The London Journal* informed readers in late October 1868 that:

> Although opened, the station on account of the magnitude of the whole and the multitude of details requiring attention in so great a work, is not yet finished; indeed, it is still very far from that condition, and anyone who visits the station will find it a scene of great activity, with swarms of skilled workmen and labourers busily engaged in all directions. The lintels of the windows in the first floor of the general offices, which close in the station and present a facade to the Euston-road, are far from complete, as well as the flank buildings along each side of the station. With the exception of something still remaining to be done in slating, glazing, and painting, the great roof, in so far as the ironwork is concerned may be said to be completed.

53   The Midland Grand and the station are listed buildings

By 1960 the former Midland Railway Hotel had fallen out of fashion and into disrepair. The hotel clock tower was clad in scaffolding. Despite now being celebrated as one of the finest examples of Victorian architecture and engineering, in the 1960s attitudes amongst architects, planners and British Rail managers were less indulgent. The hotel had become unprofitable by 1935 and following the nationalisation of the rail network after the Second World War became home to British Railways' hotel and catering offices. Along with other examples of Victorian gothic architecture, St Pancras was criticised for being little more than an old-fashioned grotesque that had lingered too long. The declining numbers using rail during the late 1950s and recommendations made in the Beeching Reports of 1963 and 1965, made St Pancras particularly vulnerable to neglect and modernising drives. In 1962 the 70ft doric arch at nearby Euston Station was torn down in spite of howls of protest from the public, and by 1966 it appeared that St Pancras was next in line for demolition. Yet the anger provoked by Euston's demolition galvanised defenders of St Pancras and British Rail found itself facing an influential alliance of critics and preservationists, led most famously by the Victorian Society. In 1967 the station and hotel were given Grade I protection (the same level of protection afforded to Canterbury Cathedral and Windsor Castle) to preserve it for the nation and force British Rail to abandon its plans for demolition.

54 The whole St Pancras complex covers more than 20 acres

Within a year of the station opening, the Midland Railway's 90,000sq.ft goods warehouse needed to be doubled in size to manage the volume of goods arriving at St Pancras. Aware of the mistakes made during the construction of Euston Station, whose Chairman lamented that the company had at great expense 'been obliged to buy streets – *streets*, gentlemen – to give the public the accommodation they require', the Midland Railway sought to 'future-proof' itself by building the Somers Town Goods Depot. With traffic continuing to grow in the 1870s, shareholders decided to construct a new goods depot next to the station along the Euston Road. Although permission to build was gained in 1875, and the land cleared in 1878, problems surrounding financing and planning meant that work did not begin until 1883. Once completed the whole station complex covered over 20 acres. An extensive network of rails connected the main station, goods yard, and various other storage facilities to the main track. In close proximity stood Somers Town's streets of terraced housing, from where many residents found work in the station or yard. On the opposite side of the track stood the Imperial Gas Light & Coke Company's gasholders.

55 The St Pancras station clock has an extraordinary span

The spirit of old Egyptian temples dwells to-day in many of the great London termini.

wrote one anonymous writer in an essay called 'The Romance of Modern London', published by *The English Illustrated Magazine* in June 1893:

[It is] dimly visible through the veil of Isis, though we call it London fog. Go at night to St Pancras, the Midland terminus, at an hour when no trains are leaving. Walk along No. 3 platform as far back as the first seat and then look back. If you are fortunate enough to catch a hidden engine belching out clouds of steam that mingle with the fog overhead – it does not need a very powerful imagination to fancy you are in some great temple. The white clouds come from the altar fire; above it, half lost in vapour, is the great clock, its huge round dial like the face of a monstrous idol before which burn in solemn stillness the hanging lamps, gleaming silver and violet and rose. Science, which built and lit this immense dome, with its span of nearly 300 feet, may not have intended to do more than construct a merely useful place, but nature will not be denied, and comes with her mysteries of light and shadow, the softening fog and the veil of night.

Opposite: Euston Station at the turn of the century. Work at Euston helped to inform the building of St Pancras. (Publishers Collection)

56   The Midland Railway's emblem is hidden around the station

Glaring down from the tops of the pillars in St Pancras station's archways are stone carvings of the legendary Wyvern. This two-legged creature was supposed to have the head and wings of a dragon, a reptilian body, and a long tail. In English folklore, it was associated with the Anglo-Saxon Kingdom of Mercia, which covered much of the Midlands. Long popular as symbols in heraldry, by the mid-nineteenth century the Wyvern had also come to be associated with industrial power. This perhaps explains why, in 1845, the Midland Railway Company adopted the Wyvern as the feature of their unofficial coat of arms and proceeded to popularise the image around their stations and trains. It appeared on luggage racks, staff uniforms, train menus, bracket signals, spandrels, and as a decorative architectural motif on the station's arches.

57   There is a hidden statue at the station

Positioned next to St Pancras' eastward-facing 270ft Clock Tower stands a 16ft-high statue of Britannia, the female personification of British national identity, gazing out across King's Cross and the north London skyline. At the time of construction, the bronze figure was just one of a plethora of statues that George Gilbert Scott incorporated into his hotel design. However, Britannia now cuts a solitary figure after the other effigies fell casualty to British Rail's cost-cutting measures in the late 1960s. For historian Michael Freeman, Britannia's presence on the station is a metaphor for the Midland Railway Company's rise to power and attempts to project a territorial command over the metropolis. Even so, the statue is easily lost amongst the intricacies of Scott's gothic spires and arches, meaning that despite its size it remains one of St Pancras's secret treasures that the everyday traveller might easily fail to spot.

58   St Pancras station's interior is designed to resemble a cathedral

The interior of St Pancras Station offers an especially beautiful example of the Neo-Gothic style of architecture. The St Pancras station booking hall, with its dark wood and vaulted ceilings, purportedly even deceived one American tourist looking for somewhere to undertake

Sunday worship, and lured by the gothic exterior, into believing that the station was in fact a church. The quatrefoil tracery inside – the symmetrical, 'four-leaved' shape of the windows – was traditionally used to represent the four Evangelists. Barlow's combination of calculated functionalism encased in a stylish aesthetic is typified by the internal brick walls, which serve no structural role but create a striking visual effect. As the journal *Fun* observed in its 'Guide to London', a decade after the station's opening, 'Coals, Burton ales, red-brick, and architecture that makes the passenger believe he is entering a desecrated cathedral chapel when he steps into a waiting room are the characteristics of the St Pancras Midland Terminus.'

Passengers would enter from the Euston Road to be greeted by porters ready to take their luggage, whilst tickets were purchased from the counter. First-class passengers enjoyed a separate booking hall that allowed them to avoid the crowds.

59   Euston Road was widened to cope with St Pancras station's traffic

Upon completion, the Somers Town Goods Depot covered an area of 14 acres and provided ample storage space for the wide variety of produce and materials transported by the Midland Railway. Although lacking the striking effect of its neighbour, the goods depot displayed careful craftsmanship in its red brickwork and arches of Mansfield Stone. Designed by The Midland Railway's Chief Engineer, John Underwood, the Depot was constructed over two levels, the upper connecting directly to the main railway line and the lower onto street level. Its building also led to the widening of the Euston Road by the Metropolitan Board of Works to cope with the increased flow of traffic. Even so, its construction came at a heavy cost for local residents with over 10,000 people forcibly displaced from their homes. Although the Midland Rail Company had agreed to enter into partnership with the Metropolitan Artisans Dwelling Company to build new 'working class houses', the project was soon in disarray, with *The Builder* remarking that 'a visit to the new spot would be sufficient to convince the most sceptical that a more dilapidated or disease ridden block of hovels does not exist in any part of the metropolis.'

Euston Road, looking west from the Wellcome. (Wellcome Library, London)

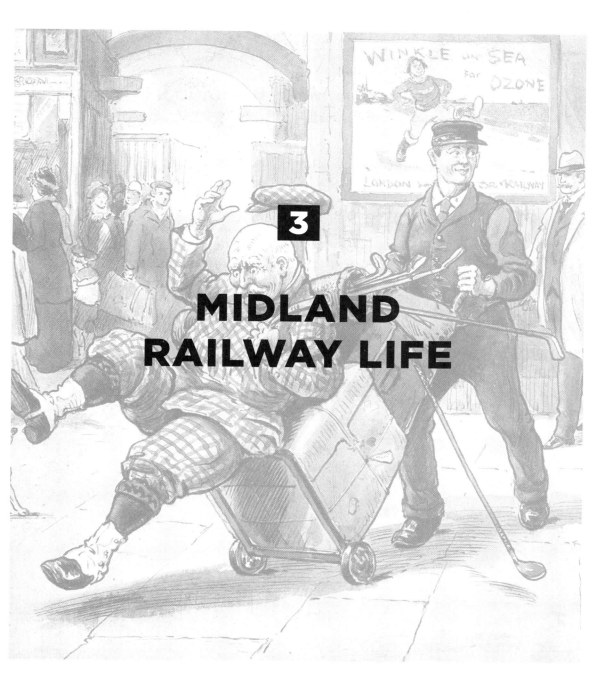

3

MIDLAND
RAILWAY LIFE

60   The space now home to the British Library was once a Midland Railway food store

For much of the period before 1914, the transportation and distribution of goods and freight was more important to the Midland Railway's commercial success than its passenger traffic. The arrival of the railways transformed the networks that kept London supplied by allowing large amounts of perishable foodstuffs to be brought fresh into the city everyday from across the country. To accommodate this traffic, the Somers Town Goods Depot, like the station itself, was built on two levels. A viaduct connected the upper level to the main line thereby allowing trains and wagons direct access, whilst the lower level was used for the storage and distribution of goods and included numerous offices rented out by suppliers. The southern section of the goods depot facing the Euston Road (now the site of the British Library) comprised a series of food and provisions stores. These included a milk and fish depot, a potato and vegetable market, and banana store. With space to handle 600 wagons at a time, the bustling distribution centre ensured easy access to Chalton Street market and for vehicles collecting supplies to be transported across London.

Once road transport replaced rail as the cheapest way to move goods around the country and coal haulage on the railways declined during the 1950s, Somers Town Goods Depot increasingly became redundant. Bomb damage sustained during the Blitz was never repaired and by the end of the 1960s the site was largely derelict. Despite significant local opposition, in 1975 the government paid £6 million for the site to become the new location for the British Library, which had outgrown its then home in the British Museum, Bloomsbury. The polarising building, which now stands next to St Pancras, was designed by the architect Colin St John Wilson and is situated on the southern part of the old goods depot. Ultimately, the construction process took over twenty years to complete and was filled with controversy throughout. When the new British Library finally opened in 1998 it became the nation's largest library and now holds a collection of over 150 million items, many of them stored deep underground. In 2015, the building was awarded the same Grade I listed status as its neighbour. The northern end of the goods yard is now occupied by the Sir Francis Crick Research Institute, built in 2011. Archaeological work undertaken at the site before construction began produced an array of finds connected to the yard, including rail tracks and the remains of the hydraulic pumping station, as well as household items from houses that were demolished in the 1880s to make way for the yard.

61   Somers Town Goods Depot had its own power station

With vast quantities of perishable foodstuffs arriving on board Midland Railway trains every day, it was essential that wagons arriving at the Somers Town Goods Depot could be quickly loaded and unloaded. Hydraulic cranes and lifts played an essential role throughout the station and goods yard. These fixed cranes, positioned along the loading platforms on upper level of the Somers Town Goods Yard, could lift 20 tons of cargo on to and off wagons. Hydraulic hoists were used to transfer wagons between levels. Prior to the advent of electrical power, the company installed a steam powered, hydraulic pumping station and pressurised water tower at the depot to power the lift and cranes. Once electric power became more widespread in the yard at the beginning of the twentieth century, a larger power station was built near Kentish Town to supply the depot and station. Even so, the depot continued to rely heavily on horses until the 1930s, with around 1,200 used to move goods around the yard and deliver items across London.

62   Somers Town Goods Depot's engineer rose to be Engineer-in-Chief to the Midland Railway

John Allen McDonald trained as a railway engineer. He was first appointed to the Midland Railway in 1871 as a Resident Engineer. One of the projects he worked on was the construction of the Somers Town Goods Depot. He subsequently served as the Midland Railway's Chief Engineer and in 1890 was appointed Engineer-in-Chief to the Company. In 1885 the construction of the Somers Town Goods Depot was getting under way; more than seventy-five men were employed on the site. Few would have worn Midland Railway uniforms, however, as most would have been labourers or foremen.

63   The Midland Railway was once London's largest supplier of coal

By far the most important and profitable commodity moved by the Midland Railway was coal, to the storage of which the northern end of the Somers Town Goods Depot was given over. By the 1880s the Midland Railway was London's largest supplier of coal, having also been the first rail company to transport inland coal to the capital. Following the construction of St Pancras, its operation quickly expanded: from transporting 156,645 tons of coal in 1866, this had increased to 1,553,000 tons by 1876, and a decade later had risen to 2,386,000 tons a year. The coal yards stretched northwards from St Pancras along the area now occupied by the Sir Francis Crick Research Institute.

Collecting coal for the Midland Railway. (Library of Congress, LC-DIG-ggbain-10366)

64   The Midland Railway became the largest in Britain

By the turn of the twentieth century, the Midland Railway had become one of the most powerful, profitable, and largest rail companies in Britain. Behind the promise of comfort, scenery and service stood an extensive and sophisticated commercial operation. In 1901, the Midland Railway owned 1,376 miles of track, carried 48,385,255 passengers and 22,442,517 tonnes of freight over a total of 47,953,527 miles. It ran 2,878 engines, 5,374 carriages, and 118,779 wagons. Off the rails, it owned 5,474 horses and 6,393 road vehicles stationed across 600 stations and depots, and employed 71,657 individuals. Overall, it expended £106,755,488 and made a profit of £11,362,932.

65   The Midland Line was one of the first to offer luxury coaches

The introduction of Britain's first luxury Pullman coaches by the Midland Railway in 1873 was a revolution in more ways than one. Firstly, they were some of the first British coaches (excluding royal and directors' saloons) to have an open-plan seating arrangement, with armchairs arranged in groups around windows and tables. Even the plushest first-class carriages of the day were still of the compartment type, whereby people sat facing each other on bench-style seats. They also introduced the first carriage heating system, the first toilets in day coaches, these previously having been limited to sleeper services, and some of the first passenger connections between coaches, albeit covered balconies as opposed to the corridors of later years. Pullmans were based on the designs pioneered in the United States by George Pullman, and it was in collaboration with his company that the Midland Railway first introduced the coaches to Britain. Soon Pullmans were being built domestically by the Pullman Car Company, founded in 1882, and supplied to most rail companies. That many of their features became commonplace on most new rolling stock in the coming years shows both how admired they were as a concept and how forward-thinking the Midland Railway was in terms of passenger comfort. Pullman services soon spread to other lines, with most major routes being able to boast one such service up until the Second World War when the number of services dropped dramatically – two cars even ran on the Metropolitan Railway out of Aldgate in the period 1910–39.

One of the most famous Victorians to travel in a Pullman car from St Pancras was Sarah Bernhardt. Born in France in 1844, by the 1890s Sarah Bernhardt was widely regarded as the most famous actress of the age. Throughout her career she performed across Europe, Britain

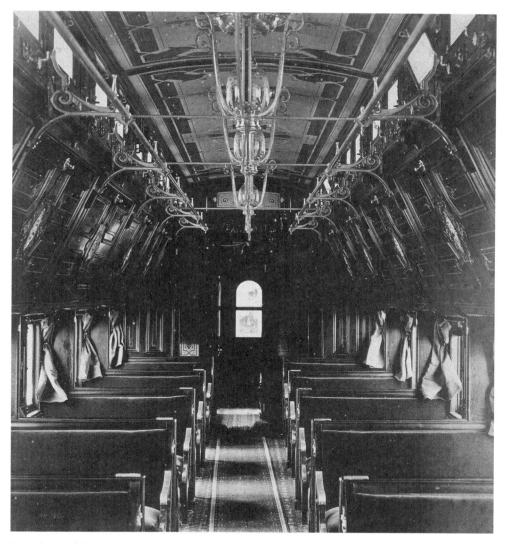

Inside a luxurious Pullman railway car in 1880. (Wellcome Library, London)

and the United States, where she also featured in early films. In the summer of 1894 she starred in a series of plays in the West End, with one reviewer lauding her as 'the divinity of the French stage'. She reached St Pancras on 28 July 1894 after a 'provincial tour' of northern cities which included one performance in Glasgow being interrupted when a male admirer invaded the stage. Throughout the tour,

she travelled in a special Midland Railway 'Pullman Palace car' and was greeted at each station by excited crowds. During this tour an American journalist asked 'how did she manage to keep so perfectly young?' 'I always burn my boats behind me,' she replied. 'What is past is past; I trouble no more about it. And the same goes regards the future. I enjoy the moment and give no thought to what may happen tomorrow.'

Sarah Bernhardt. (Library of Congress, LC-USZ62-37401)

66 Non-smoking compartments were introduced as early as 1874

The Midland Railway's early attempts to regulate rail travel on their services led to a raft of rules and regulations orders being issued by the Railway's General Manager, James Allport. These ranged from stipulating excess luggage allowance to guidelines for passengers transporting pigeons, and were dispatched to railway staff, who were expected to enforce the regulations. In Order Number 284, for example, Allport reminds Midland Railway officials that passengers smoking in non-smoking carriages had become an increasing problem and was strictly forbidden. Although acknowledging that passengers who smoke in non-designated areas were guilty of flaunting the rules, he also places blame on neglectful porters for seating non-smoking passengers in the designated smoking carriages, thereby forcing smokers to sit elsewhere. Allport draws particular attention to the practice of mistakenly seating 'ladies' in smoking carriages, something he clearly felt a Victorian lady should not be subjected to, let alone indulge in. By the time Allport retired in 1880, he had issued over 300 orders.

67 Victorian travellers had no single 'Tube map' to navigate by

At the turn of the twentieth century, London's various Underground lines were operated by competing companies, each of which produced their own maps, publicity and tickets. This meant that until *The Evening News* compiled the first 'Tube Map' in 1907 there was no single map showing the whole network. For those travelling in the 1890s, maps would have been the norm. Though these would have included stations, new routes undergoing construction, proposed routes, Omnibus routes, and overground termini, they would not have shown how each line was situated in relation to other underground lines. The District Railway had been constructed in the 1860s and was intended to facilitate train travel around an inner circle of central London by connecting to the Metropolitan Railway that ran from Paddington to St Pancras and on to the City. There was a ban on railway building in central London, so overground routes terminated at one of the capital's thirteen stations. With the introduction of underground services, from 1871 passengers arriving at St Pancras had the option of travelling onwards across London. During the first decade of the twentieth century, King's Cross St Pancras station incorporated several new deep-level routes that ran electric trains, as opposed to steam, directly under central London. By 1910, in addition to the Metropolitan & District Railway, passengers could access the Great Northern, Piccadilly & Brompton Railway (1906), which ran from Finsbury Park to Hammersmith, and the City & South London Railway (1907), which began at Euston and terminated at Clapham Common via Bank.

68 Midland Railway was the first to offer budget travel on all its trains

Rail travel was important to all social classes at the turn of the twentieth century, and 'cheap excursions' became commercially important to the Midland Railway. It allowed travellers from Yorkshire and the Midlands to enjoy festive entertainment in London, including West End pantomimes and a visit to the Crystal Palace. Working in partnership with Cook's Cheap Excursions, travellers could either stay overnight in London or return the same day. In 1872, the Midland Railway became the first rail company to open all of its trains to third-class passengers, thereby providing affordable travel to all classes.

First- and third-class carriages can be seen in this 1940 cartoon by G.H. Thompson; a rather eccentric-looking customer who cannot take his seat in the first-class carriage is arguing with a ticket controller. (Wellcome Library, London)

69   There was no second-class on the Midland Railway

From 1 January 1875 the Midland Railway became the first rail company to run only two classes of travel, first and third. While the railway drew praise and profit by improving the standard of its third-class carriages, class pretensions meant that not all travellers were so impressed.

The interior of a first-class dining car on a Midland Railway train included leather seats, heavy curtains and ornate decoration intended to conjure an atmosphere of opulent luxury, and thereby clearly differentiate first class from the sparser third-class facilities. In 1896, the Midland Railway hired Messrs Gillow, a leading firm of interior decorators who had also decorated the Midland Grand Hotel, to furnish the first-class dining car without attention to cost. Yet, as the twentieth century progressed, a growing understanding of and concern about the number of germs lurking in the furnishings meant that decoration was scaled back in the interests of hygiene. Even so, the practice of serving first-class customers a sit-down meal, replete with silver cutlery and cut glassware, persists on many long-distance services today. However, even third-class passengers travelling from St Pancras on Midland Railway express trains in November 1900 could enjoy two elaborate five-course meals for the reasonable cost of 2s for lunch and 3s for dinner. Even so, with meals prepared on board the train in cramped kitchen cars, passengers often complained that the quality of food did not match expectations. It was estimated in the 1920s that each London, Midland & Scottish Railway train required 1,510 pieces of cutlery for a full dinner service.

Even though third-class carriages lacked the ostentatious decoration of first-class saloons, the Midland Railway had long enjoyed a strong reputation for the quality and comfort of its standard service. It had been the first rail company to make a third-class service standard on all its trains and never followed the practice of several nineteenth-century rivals of placing third-class passengers in open-air wagons, which, if lucky, might contain a wooden board to sit on but were just as likely to be shared with livestock. The Midland Railway's approach proved a clever commercial move, with the company deriving substantial profits from the large number of day trippers and holidaymakers who used the railway. A corridor running down the centre allowed passengers to move between carriages whilst the train was in motion. Older designs had relied on individual compartments, which either opened directly onto the platform or joined a corridor that did not run between carriages.

70   Thomas Cook ran trips to Paris through St Pancras station from as early as 1900

One of the big beneficiaries of third-class travel was Thomas Cook & Son, whose offices had been established in Fleet Street since 1872. Travellers buying their tickets here could also purchase essential travel accessories from the incorporated shop, including luggage, guidebooks, footwear and, essential for any tourist, telescopes! Thomas Cook saw his business model as not only a social service to the hard-working Englishman, but also as a mission of religious fortitude. The relatively low cost of third-class train travel meant Cook's trips were exceedingly popular amongst the working classes, who had previously been unable to afford the high prices charged by rival tour companies. For example, one such excursion, to the Isle of Man between 20 June and 19 September 1896, offered travellers a choice of a three-, eight-, ten-, fifteen- or seventeen-day trip, with the cost of the rail fare varying between 22*s* and 26*s* depending on whether the passenger desired a cabin or a saloon car.

The Midland had worked in partnership with Thomas Cook since the 1840s, providing rail services for his rapidly expanding excursion business. Cook started out in Leicestershire when he used the Midland Line to take a group of 500, each paying 1*s*, to a temperance meeting in Leicester. His operation quickly expanded and in 1851 he organised for the Midland Railway to transport 150,000 people to visit the Great Exhibition held in Hyde Park. By the end of the century his tours had spread across the globe and were central to the start of mass tourism in Britain.

Cook *et Fils* also arranged trips from Paris to London through St Pancras. For example, the Exposition Universelle, held in Paris from April to November 1900, showcased the wonders of modern invention and technology. The Midland Railway (or *La Compagnie des Chemins de Fer Midland de l'Angleterre*) had an exhibit. Midland's agent at the exhibition was Messrs Henry Johnson & Son. The Midland Railway Company displayed its engines and carriages, alongside items such as escalators, talking films, and several 'human zoos' that claimed to show the authentic lifestyles of colonial people. Just as it had done at the 1889 Paris exhibition, the company once again won the *grand prix* for its display.

71 Before digitisation there were nearly 100,000 types of train ticket

It is easy to forget the material histories of rail travel when we look at still images of passengers and stations in the past, but these early examples of rail tickets offer a reminder of the enduring rituals of the railway. Pre-paid train tickets did not become the norm until the 1840s, following Thomas Edmondson's invention of a ticket machine that printed numbered tickets from a cardboard roll. Before the late nineteenth century trains would often stop before their station of destination so that tickets could be checked; however, by the early

twentieth century, ticket inspectors were increasingly on guard at platform barriers. These small cardboard oblongs remained the standard form for all tickets until the mid-twentieth century. Train companies produced vast stocks to cater for the volume of passengers using the railways; Simon Bradley records that, in 1933, the LMS held a stock of 300 million tickets that could be printed in any one of 90,000 types. A yellow ticket entitled the purchaser to travel third class from London to Liverpool, a journey that would have cost 16*s* 6*d* for a single and 33*s* for a return in 1911. A more colourful ticket allowed passengers to cross the channel. It remained open for a month and allowed the user to travel from Newhaven to any London terminal and then on from St Pancras.

72   Season tickets were in use as early as 1878

Season, or contract, tickets were an early introduction by the Midland Railway. They allowed passengers to avoid queuing at ticket offices and, like today, ensured a saving on the cost of travel. The conditions stipulated that the ticket must be retuned upon expiry. First-class tickets were signed by the General Manger of the Midland Railway, James Allport, and enclosed in a folding red leather wallet, which was stamped with a Midland Railway Wyvern on the inside cover.

73   In the Victorian era, dogs required a canine ticket to travel

Regulations to control passengers who brought dogs aboard Midland trains had been in place since the 1850s. In Order Number 31, delivered in November 1854, the Railway's General Manager, James Allport, instructed guards to ensure that owners travelling with dogs purchase a separate ticket for their pet. On most routes dogs would have been made to travel with the guard so to keep them away from the public carriages. However, Allport noted that there had been several recent instances of dogs being hidden in carriages to avoid payment and then escaping on to station platforms, and he reminded guards of their responsibility to confront any passengers flouting this rule. As an example, a 1896 ticket 'for one dog' travelling from St Pancras to Ashby cost 2s 6d; the Midland Railway did not relent in its attitude to canine passengers.

74   Railway tickets were once on sale in the high street

In 1923, the Conservative government passed an Act of Parliament forcing the amalgamation of the 120 independent railway companies into four private companies. The Midland Railway Company became part of the new London, Midland and Scottish Railway, which ran lines and routes throughout the north of England and across Scotland. Railway offices were a common sight in British streets, and allowed customers to book tickets or deposit goods in preparation for travel without having to visit the station. Porters would collect these items and ensure they were loaded onto the correct trains. Railway companies used their offices to advertise their services and holiday excursions, which by 1928 included tours to the First World War battlefields.

G.H Thompson cartoon from 1940, showing a porter (responsible for loading packages on to the correct train) being rather neglectful of his duty thanks to a pretty passenger. (Wellcome Library, London)

75 Midland Railway workers wore formal dress coats to work

The Midland Railway Company took great pride in the appearance of its station employees. Different uniforms were worn by a porter, signalman, ticket collector and guard respectively. Each had his role signified on his cap, underneath a Wyvern badge. The lapel insignia also illustrated rank, with the guard the most senior. All wore ties and, with the exception of the porter, frock coats. In 1905, frock coats were replaced by double-breasted jackets. The guards' caps had silver and red piping round the crown, whilst the brass buttons on each jacket gleamed brightly and bore an 'MR' insignia or displayed another Wyvern.

76 St Pancras station had a staff of 485 by the turn of the century

Adorned in the uniforms and livery of the Midland Railway Company, St Pancras station staff in the public-facing side of the station acted as guards, ticket inspectors, porters, managers, and police constables from the late Victorian era on. By 1902, the station had a staff of 485. Status and role were clearly demarcated through dress, whilst the absence of women would have reflected the dominance of male employees in the station before 1914. Wages for those working in the station at this time were slightly above the London average and depended on length of service to determine seniority: ticket examiners received between 23s and 28s per week and guards 32s to 45s; compare this with the London average pay of around 19s per week. In 1876, the stationmaster received £265 per annum, which was increased to £500 in 1897 – a figure that would have supported a comfortable middle-class lifestyle but was not amongst the highest bracket of professional salaries.

77   Victorian signals were sent by semaphore

The rapidly growing volume of traffic running into St Pancras at the start of the twentieth century necessitated a complex signalling system to manage arrivals and departures. Signal points just beyond the train shed at St Pancras Throat were used to give engine drivers instructions and information about hazards on the track. The signals were worked by wires, which ran to the signal cabin where a signalman controlled them through a series of levers. By 1900, 13,000 signal cabins were in operation across Britain's railways, with those on the same line linked by telegraph to allow communication and improve safety. The signals themselves used semaphore to communicate to drivers. Each was painted with a specific marking that gave instruction, whilst the installation of lamps in the late nineteenth century ensured they remained effective at night. Each line of track was divided into sections controlled by a set of signals, which allowed trains to be kept a safe distant apart and reduced the risk of collision. This system, which remains in use on some lines today, embodies the delicate balance between new technology and careful management by railway workers that was crucial to ensuring safety along the line.

Two banks of interlocking levers allowed the signalmen to control the busy traffic running into and out of the station and goods depot. By 1902 the station's ten tracks were controlled by forty-six signals, with 150 passenger trains entering and leaving St Pancras each day, a number that rose in the summer. This total was low compared to London's other major railway stations, with King's Cross signalmen controlling over 1,000 arrivals and departures each day. Even so, what St Pancras lacked in passenger traffic was partly made up by the number of goods trains arriving at Somers Town Goods Depot.

78   St Pancras station used old-style lever signals until 1957

St Pancras junction's new signalling station, installed in 1957, formed part of the ongoing modernisation drive on British railways. Gone were the interlocking levers of the pre-war days, replaced with an electronic system of coloured lights, which was easier to operate and simpler for drivers to understand. Rail authorities wanted to improve congestion around the station, particularly for passenger services, and ensure greater safety on an increasingly busy line. The new signal box was praised by *The Railway Gazette* for providing staff with every amenity for their comfort, including a new console with over 250 switches. The illuminated diagram above the console covered sixty-four sections of track and was lit by a series of lamps to show where each train stood on the track. With the turning of a single switch, one signalman could now control all the points required to set a train in motion.

79   The Midland Railway was one of the first to make food available to customers during their journeys

In a 1903 railway travel guide, written by a journalist at *The Times* and entitled *The Complete Railway Traveller*, readers were reminded:

> That the traveller shall be conveyed in safety and will all possible speed to his destination is the first duty of every railway. But in the case of a railway that aspires to be an agent of travel in the fullest sense of the word its duty is not wholly comprised of mere mechanical transport of passengers. It has also obligations in the provision of travelling comforts *en route*, and of food and refreshment at the starting place and intermediate stations, or, in the case of long distance journeys, on the train itself.

During the late nineteenth century, the Midland Railway enjoyed a reputation for providing such service and for pioneering novel contraptions to improve passengers' experience. One such innovation was the introduction of platform food carts, such as the one seen here, which were wheeled alongside the train during stops to allow passengers to purchase food through the carriage windows. Decorated with a crown of foliage, these carts included a gas heater to keep food warm and a glass cabinet to protect items from the grime of the station. Once carriage design was improved to allow passengers to move between along and between coaches by a central corridor, so refreshment carts moved onto the train itself.

80   The Midland Railway used to issue commemorative knives to its passengers

Commemorative penknives represent one of the odd knick-knacks of mid-twentieth-century rail travel. Encased in an embossed leather wallet, they were issued to passengers aboard the inaugural British Railways Midland Pullman service on the 4 July 1960. This new luxury service travelled daily from St Pancras to Manchester along the Midland Main Line in a record-breaking time of three hours and fifteen minutes. The train included two on-board kitchens, and provided a full meal service at every seat, although it is not clear why passengers were given a penknife. Ultimately, the Midland Pullman did not last long, being replaced in 1966 by an electric locomotive that ran from Manchester to Euston along the West Coast Mainline.

81   The trip from London to Glasgow once took ten hours

Guests attending the The London, Tilbury and Southend Railway Locomotive, Carriage, Wagon and Marine Departments 15th Annual Beanfeast were treated to a sumptuous meal, detailed on a menu printed on a card booklet with yapp edges, during their journey from St Pancras to Scotland. The trip took place on 2 July 1909, with guests travelling from London St Pancras to Glasgow and then on to Balloch to spend an afternoon enjoying a steamer excursion on Loch Lomond. The five-course menu on offer for Saturday's dinner appears somewhat grander than the meals available in first class today but came at the very reasonable price of 2s 6d per head. Another page in the booklet showed the itinerary and timetable for the weekend, with the train due to depart at 9.30 p.m. from London St Pancras and arriving in Glasgow at 7.30 a.m. the following day. The ten-hour journey was most efficient by 1909 standards, although today the same journey can be accomplished in just four hours and thirty-two minutes. The booklet also included an amusing thirty-seven-page fictionalised 'almanac' detailing imaginary events that would take place during the three-day excursion, presumably for travellers to enjoy during the long journey.

82   Midland Railway workers joined the General Strike of 1926

St Pancras railwaymen went out on strike during the General Strike of May 1926. From 4 May to 12 May, between 1.5 and 1.75 million workers, across a wide variety of industries and all over Britain, came out on strike in support of coal miners after colliery owners tried to enforce a 13 per cent pay cut and an extension of working hours. Industrial relations had deteriorated during the early 1920s as Britain's heavy industry struggled to recover from the effects of the First World War and post-war scarcity continued to afflict the lives of working-class communities across Britain. The General Strike created havoc across the country, with the government resorting to using troops at the London docks and recruiting volunteer policemen and train drivers to keep essential services running. At one stage, the Cabinet even considered taking over the BBC so as to control the flow of information. Support for the strike proved to be particularly enthusiastic around St Pancras, where there the Communist Party had a strong presence. On 4 May one meeting outside the York Road Goods Depot drew 2,000 railwaymen, and on the night of 9 May police raided the headquarters of the St Pancras Communist Party, seizing stationery and 'one typewriter' in an attempt to quell its activities!

83   The Midland 4-2-2 was one of the finest engines ever built

Artist and railway enthusiast Cuthbert Hamilton Ellis is just one of the painters to capture the Midland Railway's 4-2-2 locomotive (in his case, painting the No. 614 gathering steam as it leaves St Pancras). Born in 1909, Ellis was an avid railway writer, publishing over thirty books on the subject by the time he was 30. His paintings and descriptions of steam travel, mostly produced as the age of steam was coming to an end, evoke a romantic and nostalgic pleasure for an earlier period. The 4-2-2 express engine was designed by S.W. Johnson and represents one of the engineering glories of the Victorian age. Appointed Midland Railway Locomotive Superintendent in 1873, Johnson pioneered a new design of engine that increased efficiency and speed. First introduced in 1887, by 1900 ninety-five of these engines were in service on Midland lines. The 4-2-2 express could travel at over 90mph and pull up to 300 tons. While a few remained in use until the 1930s, most of the 4-2-2s started to be scrapped in the early 1920s.

Midland Railway Express Locomotive No. 117, designed by Mr. Samuel Johnson, Locomotive Superintendent. (Wellcome Library, London)

84   The first passenger diesel locomotive ran from St Pancras station

Although relatively common in continental Europe and the USA since the early 1930s, prior to the Second World War the use of diesel in Britain was limited to a small number of shunting locomotives. However, after the resolution of the conflict thoughts turned to modernising the UK's rail network, with the logical solution for the many routes being the introduction of diesel locomotives as a direct replacement for steam. The first example of this was on the London Midland & Scottish Railway (LMS), who outshopped the country's first main-line diesel locomotive, No. 1000, in December 1947. The timing was significant as the company was absorbed into the nationalised British Railways only a few weeks later. The locomotive undertook its first loaded test runs on 14 and 15 January 1948 between St Pancras and Manchester, keeping to schedules designed for the LMS's standard 4-6-0 express locomotives. Once in full service, No. 1000 and its twin No. 1001 (outshopped in July 1948) worked a variety of routes out of St Pancras and Euston, both singly and in pairs – though as non-standard designs of only modest power they were quickly superseded by later British Railways diesels, and both were withdrawn by 1966.

In an effort to reduce running costs and improve efficiency, British Railways initiated a 'Modernisation Plan' in 1955 intended to introduce diesel-powered trains across the network. Diesel Multiple Units quickly replaced steam-hauled sets on suburban routes running into and out of St Pancras, and proved popular with the rapidly growing number of commuters travelling into London for work. Diesel services provided a faster and cleaner travelling experience for passengers, who would no longer had to contend with the cloud of soot produced by steam engines. By the 1960s more than 200,000 people who lived over 12 miles away from central London were commuting into the city on

overground services each day. This not only increased the volume of people moving through St Pancras but also saw a change in the type of person most frequently using the station.

85   'Britain's Most Exciting Train' ran from St Pancras station

By 1960, the railways were experiencing heavy losses in passenger traffic to cars and the emerging domestic airlines. One of British Railways' many ideas to lure back custom was the introduction of the Blue Pullman – a luxury, high-speed diesel service running between London and the Midlands or Manchester, designed to attract businessmen travelling at their company's expense. It was billed as 'Britain's most exciting train', not only proving that fixed-length diesel units were viable, thus paving the way for the high-speed trains of the 1970s, but also redefining luxury travel. Whereas old steam-hauled Pullmans reeked of antiquated grandeur, the new trains were sleek and stylish, with modern interiors built using the latest materials. And yet some vestiges of the old services remained: the silver service, the white-jacketed attendants, and, crucially for British Railways, the supplementary fare.

Midland Pullman services operated out of St Pancras to various destinations using the Blue Pullman sets from July 1960 until 1966, when the line between Euston and Manchester was electrified, shortening journey times such that the Midland route could not keep up. The Blue Pullmans were subsequently sent to the Western Region and were withdrawn by 1973, standard coaching stock improvements enabling better value for money on regular fares.

86 St Pancras station pioneered a new type of train that never ran

The British Rail prototype APT-E (Advanced Passenger Train Experimental), the first high-speed tilting train to run in Britain. Against a background of rising competition from cars and domestic airlines, high-speed rail services began to appear across Europe in the 1970s. Development of the APT-E began in 1970 and the train first ran in 1972, with tests taking place along the Midland Line from Leicester to St Pancras, a journey it could complete in under an hour. Among the APT-E's novel features were articulated bogies (bogies shared between coaches), gas turbine generators to power the traction motors rather than diesel, and a tilt function. At 70m long and made from aluminium, the APT-E set a new railway speed record, reaching 152.3mph during testing. The train, however, never made it into regular service. Disputes with ASLEF over the single operator's chair dogged the project from the start (previously all trains had two seats in the cab), whilst a growing focus on electrification, rising fuel costs, and declining budgets meant that immediately upon completing testing in 1976 the APT-E was retired to the National Railway Museum at York. Although its speed record was soon beaten, and those who travelled on it were limited to a few British Rail employees and VIPs, its technology became crucial to the introduction of regular high-speed services on to Britain's railways during the 1980s, as well as to the development of the high-speed services seen at St Pancras station today.

87 Trains to run here include a working replica of Rocket

In March 1980 crowds at St Pancras were treated to a celebration of railway history when a replica of George Stephenson's *Rocket* steamed into the station. Built in 1829 for the Rainhill Trials, *Rocket* went on to become one of the first locomotives on the Liverpool & Manchester Railway and the first to carry both passengers and mail. The original is on display in the Science Museum but this one was built by the National Railway Museum in 1979 for the 'Rocket 150' events. To mark the 150th anniversary and the release of the Post Office's accompanying set of commemorative stamps, the locomotive undertook a mile-and-half-long journey from Cambridge Street Depot to St Pancras. Five first-class stamps depicting early rail travel were issued, each costing 12p!

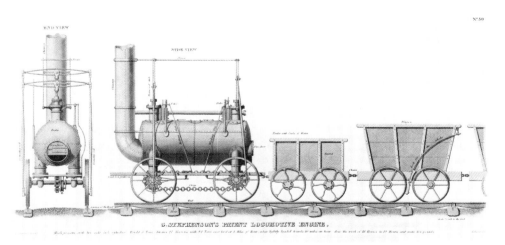

The Rocket. (Library of Congress, LC-USZ62-110386)

88   Dockers, miners and all three rail unions came out on strike during 1972

The opening months of 1972 witnessed strikes across British industry, with both the dockers and miners coming out on strike following disputes over pay and working practices. On 13 April 1972, the three main rail unions rejected an 11 per cent pay offer from British Rail and declared a work-to-rule. Even though, Edward Heath's Conservative government initially refused to meet the rail union demands, following a month marked by ever worsening delays and disruptions the government backed down and agreed a 13 per cent pay deal, which required a special £27 million grant to ensure the resumption of normal service. One of the many rail offers to resume was British Rail's Merry-Maker excursions. Started in the late 1960s, they offered cheap Sunday day trips to the coast and other places of interest. By 1980, over 480,000 travellers had experienced a Merry-Maker excursion.

89 British Railways took over management of St Pancras station in the 1950s

By the late 1980s passengers approaching or departing St Pancras looked out upon a very different landscape to that seen even a decade before. An intricate web of overhead electric wires and cables illustrated the profound changes in railway technology since the replacement of steam trains in the late 1950s. On 1 January 1948, the four private rail companies were nationalised and amalgamated as British Railways, which also took over the running of St Pancras station. One effect of nationalisation was to create far greater standardisation of engines and infrastructure across the rail network. Electric rail had first appeared in the 1880s, but it was not until the late 1950s that British Railways started to systematically introduce overhead electric lines across the over ground system. The Midland Main Line from St Pancras to Bedford, originally built upon for the opening of the station, was electrified in 1983.

4

THE STATION AT WAR

90   Midland Railway employees fought in the First World War

During the First World War, 22,941 Midland Railway employees served in Britain's armed forces. Of these 2,833 were killed in service and a further 7,068 wounded. Due to the importance of railway work to the war effort, those wanting to enlist had to get special permission from their stationmaster. George Albert Walker, a 'van man' at St Pancras, was one such employee. His permission was issued in November 1915. Although little else is known of Walker, it is likely that he was the same George Albert Walker who appears in the 1911 census as living in Pemberton Terrace, just off the Holloway Road, with his wife, Bessie, and three young children, Gladys, Ellaline, and George Edmund. Born in parish of St Pancras in 1872, Walker had been in the employ of the Midland Railway since at least 1901, when he was listed on the census as a railway porter, and by 1911 he had become an omnibus driver for the railway company.

The Midland Railway promised to find work for all those who wanted it after the war. George Walker survived but the names of those Midland Railway employees who did not are recorded on a 31ft cenotaph designed by Sir Edwin Lutyens and erected at the company's headquarters in Derby. In addition, the company published a memorial volume, which records, over sixty-five pages, the names and details of those who died. The memorial was unveiled by Charles Booth, the Midland Railway Chairman, three years after the end of the war on 15 December 1921, in a ceremony attended by large numbers of families who had lost a relative. Surmounted by a sarcophagus upon which is the rested figure of a soldier, the cenotaph bears the inscription, 'To the brave men of the Midland Railway Company who gave their lives in the Great War'.

91   The first American ambulance train sent to the front in the First World War was inspected at St Pancras station

Visitors to St Pancras station on New Year's Eve 1917 would have been greeted by the sight of the American Army's first ambulance train, built by the Midland Railway at its works in Derby, awaiting inspection before being despatched to the Western Front. The carriages were filled with banks of bunks, which the *Illustrated London News* observed had 'been planned to ensure the greatest possible ease and comfort for the occupants'.

Ambulance trains had been used by the British throughout the war to transport the wounded away from the front and back to Britain. Patients were cared for by teams of nurses, doctors, and also conscientious objectors, who would often travel to areas of heavy fighting at the front in order to collect casualties. The bunks positioned over three levels were welded to the side of the train and secured with steel wires to the floor and ceiling of each carriage. US troops first saw action on the Western Front in October 1917, and by June 1918 were arriving at a rate of 10,000 a day. By the end of the war 2 million US servicemen were stationed in Europe, with the American Army suffering 320,000 casualties.

Inside an American ambulance train. (Wellcome Library, London)

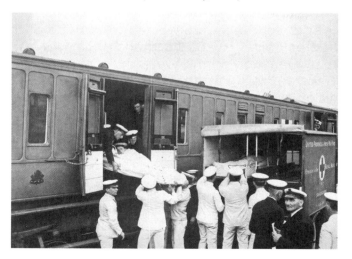

Loading up an ambulance train at Chatham. (Wellcome Library, London)

92   St Pancras station was bombed during the First World War

Although memories of the Blitz have tended to dominate accounts of wartime bombing in London, the city faced a similar threat during the First World War after Germany launched a strategic bombing campaign using Zeppelin airships. Over fifty raids took place, mainly at night, with 5,000 bombs dropped and 835 people dying between 1915 and 1918. Railway tracks and stations quickly became principal targets, leading the government to provide the Midland Railway with detailed instructions on what to do in the event of an attack. Although the railways remained beyond military control during day-to-day operations, when the call 'take air raid action!' was issued trains on the rails had to draw all blinds, run at 15mph for passenger trains and 10mph for goods trains, and reduce steam. Maps were used to coordinate the Railway's response: the country was divided into numbered sections, with those in danger of daylight raids coloured red. When an air raid warning was made, head office in Derby would inform all stations in a given area to take precautions.

St Pancras station itself suffered badly during a raid on the night of 17 February 1918 when five bombs fell around the station and hotel, killing twenty people and injuring a further thirty-three. Sections of the glass roof were destroyed when one bomb fell near the booking office and three more fell on the hotel, causing £4,345 worth of damage and killing four members of staff. Despite the loss of life, train services continued uninterrupted.

93 Many women worked on the railways during the First World War

22,941 Midland Railway employees (40 per cent of the company's workforce) joined the armed services during the First World War. To keep the railway system running, the company depended upon large numbers of female workers to fill the vacant positions and by 1918 employed nearly 9,000 women. Throughout the war, their contribution was vital to ensuring troops, casualties, munitions and supplies continued to move around the rail network. Some were employed as porters at the Somers Town Goods Depot, who were responsible for moving luggage and goods between the yard and the platforms. After the war, most women employed by the Midland Railway lost their jobs as men returned from the forces and went straight back into their previous positions.

94 First World Troops often arrived home through St Pancras station

Marching in full regimental order, the 2nd Grenadier Guards left St Pancras station en route to their barracks in Chelsea following their return from fighting on the Western Front during the First World War. The Guards had sailed from Dunkirk to Tilbury, before catching a special train to St Pancras, where they were welcomed by a large, expectant crowd of family members, friends and onlookers. Yet, even as the regimental band began to play, *The Times* reported that this was an occasion marked not by elaborate ceremony and jubilant colour but rather, 'just a home-coming and when the train appeared the returning warriors quickly made it evident that so they regarded the event ...

It was all matter-of-fact and eminently British.' As the reporter made clear, 'everybody must have been conscious that the Grenadiers now returning were not those who left England in the autumn of 1914. The great majority of the original battalion had been left behind. Another kind of glory was theirs – the glory of those who die for a country and a cause.' But then, as the troops began to march down the station ramp, the band commenced 'Old Comrades' and the Guards 'met the multitude which was waiting to greet them and the spell was broken. A roar burst from the throng – suddenly as though a seal had snapped. It came from the yard of the station in a volume of reverberating sound. London had indeed found its voice.'

95   General Sir Ian Hamilton hosted a ceremonial burning of vermin in Somers Town

In 1924, a young Church of England priest named Father Basil Jellicoe, who had been working at the Magdalen Mission in Somers Town founded the St Pancras House Improvement Society with the aim of ripping down Somers Town's decrepit nineteenth-century tenements and replacing them with modern flats. He was closely supported by Irene Barclay, Britain's first professionally qualified chartered surveyor and the Society's secretary, whose research into the area's poor housing during the 1920s was key to raising awareness and funds for the redevelopment plan. The charity's ambition to create a 'miniature garden city' in Somers Town attracted support from numerous prominent figures, including the Queen, Prince of Wales and members of the London County Council. To mark the start of building on the St Christopher's flats and in celebration of the Society's sixth anniversary, a large crowd of local residents and dignitaries gathered to watch as General Sir Ian Hamilton, commander of British forces during the disastrous Gallipoli campaign in 1915, lit a ceremonial bonfire, topped by models of bedbugs and lice, on 29 January 1931. Efforts to improve children's health by providing antiseptic washes to kill the lice endemic in many homes had been undertaken by the St Pancras Cleaning Station since 1910; however, the Housing Improvement Society stressed the need for modern housing to replace the vermin-infested nineteenth-century tenements and used this as an opportunity to raise public awareness of their project.

General Sir Ian Hamilton. (Library of Congress, LC-DIG-ggbain-18025)

96 St Pancras had to cancel its Continental travel offers on the outbreak of the Second World War

In 1939, the London, Midland & Scottish Railway had boards up across the station promoting their rail services to France, promising holidays for all seasons, in city and countryside. They offered 'sea and sunshine' on the Riviera, 'mountains, sun and snow' in the French Alps and art and history tours across 'Roman and Medieval France'. Such adverts, commonly seen around St Pancras and other stations, offered rail connections from the Midlands, north of England and Scotland to the Southern Railway's boat trains that left from Victoria and crossed to France at Dover. Smaller posters promoted other travel services, including the London, Midland & Scottish Railway's baggage insurance. Following the outbreak of war in September 1939, however, and Germany's invasion of France the following May, Continental travel soon became impossible.

97   In 1939, troops arriving at St Pancras station were welcomed by the Halo hairnet girl

Second World War train information noticeboards contained a large space in the centre for advertising. Situated in the middle of the St Pancras station information board in 1939, troops leaving for the Continent at the beginning of the Second World War were greeted with a large advert for Halo silk hairnets, which promised them that 'There's a Halo net for every hair need', day or night. The mass-produced nets were made of art silk and available at high-street stores, including Boot's chemists, for 2s. The popularity of hair nets grew massively during the interwar period as women looked to protect bobbed or curled hairstyles when wearing hats or sleeping. Adverts for such products illustrate the efforts made by companies to target women consumers but also the way advertising artists, almost always men, depicted a very particular vision of womanhood. Placed between the arrivals and departure boards, the adverts occupied a prime location in the station, but also ensured any troops reading the message on the board instructing them to report to the Railway Transport Office would be greeted by a smiling 'haloed' image.

Opposite: 7 September 1939, and a Whitehall newspaper seller announces the outbreak of war. (Library of Congress, C-USZ62-132594)

98   The Second World War resulted in significant delays for civilian passengers on British rail lines

A glance at the St Pancras station arrivals board in 1943 would have offered a snapshot of travel chaos. Temperatures were particularly cold that December, dropping to -7°C, and many trains from the north ran significantly late. For the duration of war the railways were brought under government control to ensure the efficient movement of troops, supplies and weapons; however, this frequently led to passenger services being delayed or cancelled.

99   18,000 Belgian refugees came through St Pancras station during the Second World War

In May 1940, thousands of young Belgian refugees disembarked at St Pancras station. They had fled to Britain following Nazi Germany's invasion of Belgium on the 10 May. Many arrived in London on board trains, carrying only a few belongings hurriedly bundled together. Much of the responsibility for welcoming and housing the refugees fell on voluntary organisations, such as the Women's Voluntary Services for Civil Defence, which established a series of War Refugee Committees across the country. Requests were placed in the press for people to welcome refugees into their homes or to donate clothes and other useful household items. Around 60 per cent of the refugees remained in London, with the rest spreading across the country. Even though numbers were far smaller than initially expected, the welcome extended was not always warm; local residents feared that refugees would receive preferential treatment in the search for work and welfare, while King Leopold III's surrender of Belgium forces at the end of May stoked fears that some arrivals might be Nazi agents. Over the next five years, the Belgian community built a strong associational network, establishing clubs and churches, whilst their children integrated into local schools across Britain. At the end of the war, the majority of refugees returned to Belgium, with many departing from St Pancras to return home.

100   St Pancras station was a target during the Second World War

St Pancras' distinctive architecture and importance as a transport hub made it a prime target for Luftwaffe bombers during the Blitz, which ran from September 1940 to May 1941. The station was hit several times during the war. During a raid on 10–11 May 1941, five bombs fell on the station. The burnt-out wreckage of trains littered the platforms, whilst the roof suffered serious damage that remained unrepaired until after the war. That night's raids were some of the heaviest London experienced during the Blitz, with bombs also

A little boy sits in the ruins after a raid on London. (Library of Congress, LC-DIG-ppmsca-19004)

hitting the Houses of Parliament, the British Library and Westminster Abbey. In its report of the bombing, *The Times* praised the 'magnificent efforts of the armed and civil defences', noting that thirty-three German aircraft had been shot down: 'Here was another exhibition of the spirit of the national defence – a defence of the people by the people – a defence of city and home and freedom'. On the same night, German cities experienced similar destruction as the RAF carried out its own bombing raids across Hamburg and Berlin. Despite the wreckage, St Pancras closed for only one week, whilst Platforms 2 and 3 were operational again within a month.

St Paul's wreathed in smoke during an air raid, December 1940. (Library of Congress, LC-USZ62-61239)

101 There were concerts in St Pancras Underground during the Second World War

Many Londoners struggled to find moments of relief, entertainment and escape during the wartime Blitz. Nightly bombing raids by the German Luftwaffe necessitated the construction of underground shelters, and while those with sufficient space may have had a shelter in their home or garden, most Londoners relied upon the cellars of large buildings or Underground stations. In an effort to maintain morale, authorities organised subterranean theatre performances and variety shows to entertain those sheltering during the bombing. Although opportunities for public entertainment were circumscribed during the Second World War, it did not prevent a peak of 25 to 30 million cinema tickets being sold as audiences enjoyed blockbusters such as *Gone With The Wind*, whilst the government established the Council for the Encouragement of Music and the Arts to support cultural endeavours during the war. These shows provided an important break for war-weary Londoners; even as bombing raids drove concerts and theatre productions underground, public enthusiasm for these important pastimes did not subside.

Above ground, St Pancras Borough Council Theatre Company provided free musical and theatrical entertainment to help maintain morale. Building its stage in the area's bomb-damaged streets, the company performed a variety of shows, including some by local residents, in a different street every night. As *The Daily Mirror* proclaimed when it published a story about a performance in Hartfield Road, Chalk Farm: 'All the boro's a stage ... with window boxes, an upper circle on the sills and a promenade.'

102   Crews of women swept St Pancras's streets after every air raid

With many male workers enlisting in the armed forces during the Second World War, large numbers of women entered the workforce to take their place. Mrs G. Warren of the St Pancras Women's Street Cleaning Brigade was just one of the women to sweep the area's streets in 1942. Bomb-damaged buildings testified to the destruction caused by German raids. Around 20,000 Londoners died and over 1 million homes were destroyed during the Blitz, with the area around St Pancras and Somers Town hit fifty-four times. One resident of Somers Town, who was a child during the war, later recalled:

My father had a shoe repair shop in Somers Town during the war and we lived over the shop. One night during the blitz the front windows and door were blown out and there was a scramble of looters helping themselves to shoes, polish, lasts, anything in fact that they could carry away. My father and the air-raid wardens put a stop to that! But, even with the house boarded up my dad would not go down to the shelter although my mum, my two brothers, my sister and I went every night to the tube with our 'bundle' consisting of a small eiderdown to lie on, we slept on the floor on the platform until, later on in the war we were allocated bunks. The station we sheltered in was Leicester Square because Mum said our nearest one, King's Cross, was too rough! We also took a large flask of cocoa and some mugs. I was five when the war started and, to this day, the sound of the air-raid warning sends a chill up my spine.

Opposite: An Underground shelter in London. Activities held underground included concerts. (Library of Congress, LC-USZC4-4337)

Yet, as the efforts of the Cleaning Brigade highlights, something of a 'Blitz spirit' did emerge: every morning female street cleaners, like Mrs Warren, would sweep the streets to keep them clean and accessible for traffic. To deal with the damage created by the bombing a force of 8,700 Pioneer Corps military personnel and a 10,000-strong civilian force cleared debris and repaired roads from October 1940 onwards.

103   Women cleaned the station's engines during the wars

As had been the case during the First World War, women once again entered all sections of the workforce after 1939, fulfilling essential roles in keeping industry and the railways running during the war. Female workers cleaned the steam engines in St Pancras Cleaning Yard. Cliff Rowe was one wartime painter who captured this in action. Born in Wimbledon into a working-class family in 1904 and a committed communist for much of his life, Rowe used his art to capture the dignity of labour, and the relationship between workers and machines as the basis of industrial society. In 1934, he founded the radical Artists International Association, which undertook anti-fascist and anti-imperial campaigns, and later produced publicity material for the Attlee government, Trade Union movement and posters for the 1951 Festival of Britain. In his image, the female worker, dressed in work overalls and dwarfed by the engine, calmly completes the intricate task of cleaning the engine's steam tubes. To prevent the build-up of ash and keep engines running at maximum efficiency they needed to be cleaned every two weeks. The workers blasted steam into the tubes to flush out residual dirt using a steam lance. Rowe is one of the People's History Museum's 100 Radical Heroes.

104   Many evacuees left London from St Pancras station

Evacuation became an enduring memory of the Second World War for many of London's children. St Pancras was often the starting point for journeys to rural areas believed to be safer than remaining in the city. Although the worst of the bombing hit during the Blitz of 1940–41, when 25 per cent of London's residents left the city, air raids resumed in the summer of 1944 with Germany's development of the new V-weapons – the V-1 flying bomb, or Doodlebug, and the V-2 rocket. A fresh wave of evacuations saw 1.5 million people depart London that summer. The National Fire Service helped evacuees board trains to be transported north. One evacuee who left from St Pancras later recalled being taken to the station in buses, before lining-up on the platform waiting for the train to arrive and eating his by then squashed fruit and melted chocolate that he had been given for the journey.

A month after VE-Day, some of the first evacuees to arrive home in London following the end of the war in Europe arrived at the station. Newspapers across the country celebrated the happy homecoming of those on board the first of the 'Homeward Specials', which arrived at St Pancras from Leicester at 12.12 p.m. on 4 June 1945: 68 mothers, 172 children, 47 'priorities', four of whom were blind, 13 London County Council escorts, a train marshal, luggage marshal and four Women's Volunteers Service welfare officers tumbled onto the platform to be greeted by Mrs Cynthia Willink, wife of the Minister of Health. Many of the children brought wartime pets back with them, with *The Birmingham Mail* reporting, 'Happy smiling children, waving flags and carrying pets, including dogs, cats, kittens and birds in cages, enlivened St Pancras station today.' These were the first of 3,500 arrivals to return to the capital aboard Homeward Specials. The youngest passenger on this train was just 7 weeks old, whilst the eldest, an 81-year-old blind evacuee, cheered, 'There's no place like home'.

105 Thanks to its key logistical role in the war, the station was the site of many happy reunions

More than sixty years before Paul Day's statue was installed at the head of St Pancras station's platforms, *The Sunday People* reported another happy reunion in the station that produced a familiar pose. On 2 December 1944 a 'Christmas leave special' train arrived at St Pancras carrying 500 soldiers back from the Italian front. Fred and Edith Wells were there reunited for the first time in three years. Along with his fellow passengers, Fred had won a leave lottery that entitled to him twenty-eight days at home over Christmas. The newspaper reported that 'golden haired, 4ft tall' Mrs Wells said, 'this is the first lottery we have ever won'. As family members stood 'tip-toed' on the platform, the soldiers tumbled out of the train in excitement to greet their loved ones, while a second train that had been delayed by three hours arrived almost empty after many soldiers disembarked early in an attempt to get back quicker. Unfortunately, the final serviceman to leave the train headed to hospital rather than home after he fell and sprained his knee in the excitement.

Opposite: A group of East End evacuees at dinner. (Library of Congress, LC-USW33-000862-C)

106   The Government banned 'special excursion services' during the war

Excited Derby County fans filled St Pancras station's platforms as they arrived in London for the February 1948 FA Cup Quarter Final tie with Queens Park Rangers. Despite an association with football hooliganism in the 1970s and 80s, 'football special trains' had carried supporters around the country on matchdays since the early twentieth century. 28 February 1948 saw one of the first 'Football Specials' following the government's lifting of the wartime ban on special excursion services. In one press image, Derby fan Miss Gwynne Wheldan was photographed shaking hands with the train fireman, George Abbott, while other supporters, sporting their team's black and white rosettes, waved the rattles that generated one of the defining sounds of post-war football. After seeing their side draw 1-1 at QPR's Shepherds Bush stadium, Derby fans enjoyed a 5-0 win in the reply at the Baseball Ground a week later.

5

INTERESTING FACTS ABOUT THE STATION

107 The first train to arrive at St Pancras station was the 4.20 a.m. Leeds Mail

The station opened with surprisingly little fanfare and generated negligible press coverage. At 4.20 a.m. on the morning of 1 October 1868, the overnight Leeds Mail trundled into the station to become the first arrival at St Pancras station. The lack of occasion is explained by the Midland Railway's desperate need to start generating revenue from the station even before it was completed or the Midland Grand Hotel built: by autumn 1868 the construction was worryingly behind schedule and significantly over budget, leaving the Midland Railway financially overstretched. Writing in the late 1960s, historian Jack Simmons observed the irony of this anticlimactic beginning:

> The Company had worked so hard, for six years, to secure its own access to London; and when that access had been achieved, instead of proclaiming, with a flourish of trumpets, that it had arrived in the capital, it slipped in almost unobserved. As the Midland clerks moved their stock of tickets and equipment over from King's Cross in the small hours, the Company's entry seemed most to resemble that of a thief in the night.

108 When it opened, St Pancras station had only two platforms

Despite its size, upon opening in 1868, St Pancras station contained only two platforms: one for arrivals and the other for departures, with the area in between used to store engines and rolling stock. Amongst the steam and dirt of Victorian railway stations, visitors would have been presented with a busy station scene: labourers working on the tracks next to a rail cart holding large iron girders; crowds waiting on the platforms to board trains or hail horse-drawn cabs. Beyond the large iron and glass screen, designed to protect the interior of the station from the weather, the Imperial Gas Light & Coke Company's gasholders and station signal cabin framed the approach to the station.

Today, St Pancras comprises four stations merged into one: the Eurostar terminus; high-speed services to Kent; East Midland Trains and Thameslink services that run north on the old Midland Railway line; all standing on top of six London Underground lines. St Pancras' elaborate nineteenth-century structure has been reimagined and redeveloped to suit its role as a twenty-first-century hub for domestic and international rail travel, through which 45 million rail passengers pass each year. While preserving the core structure, the original brick- and ironwork, and other key design features, the station has been doubled in length and incorporated six new platforms to serve the increased volume of trains. The famous glass roof remains intact, providing natural light throughout the station, while several of the original blind arches on the upper level have been opened up to create space for new retail and food units. Four large lightwells inserted into the platform deck allow easy access between the original platform level and what was Barlow's beer store below. The old undercroft is now a retail centre, housing various station facilities, such as ticket offices, cafes, high street retailers and independent shops.

109   Eurostar runs from Midland Railway's original Victorian platforms

Running at 186mph across a series of high-speed rail lines, the sleek Class 373/1 engines of the Eurostar service exemplify the technological sophistication and speed of modern rail travel. At 387m long, comprising eighteen carriages, and capable of carrying 750 passengers, the Eurostar service connects London to Europe through St Pancras station. The completion of the Channel Tunnel in 1994 made possible for the first time an uninterrupted rail journey from London to the continent. Initially run from Waterloo, Eurostar moved to St Pancras following its redevelopment in September 2007. Passengers today still board the service along the same platforms that welcomed the Midland Railway's steam engines in 1868 but upon leaving the station can be in Paris in just over two hours – a journey lasting under half the time it took to reach Derby in the early twentieth century.

110   The Eurostar has featured on the cover of Britain's oldest railway magazine

Throughout its history, railway travel has exercised a strong pull on the public imagination. Numerous books, paintings, and later films and television programmes stand as testament to a wider popular fascination with train travel. From the late nineteenth century, a more specialist literature started to emerge that catered to the wide audience of amateur enthusiasts who created a diverse range of forums and pastimes in which to share their passion. First published in July 1897 by Joseph Lawrence and Frank Cornwell, *The Railway Magazine* is the oldest and most popular such magazine in Britain. Edited by George Augustus Noakes, under the pseudonym G. A. Sekon, it quickly built a monthly following of 25,000 and coined phrases such as 'railwayac' and 'locomotivac'. Continuing today, each monthly edition provides in-depth articles and images ranging across a wide array of railway-related topics.

111   St Pancras railway workers were once photographed by a missionary

Reverend John Galt worked as a missionary in the East End for the London City Mission. He was a keen photographer, taking thousands of photos intended to capture the poverty of London's streets. Some survive in the form of a plate lantern slide, which Galt used to illustrate various lectures he gave to raise awareness and money for his mission work. His photographs included one of a railway maintenance gang working on the line just outside St Pancras station. Tracks required careful upkeep to ensure that the bullhead rails did not come loose and that the points remained well lubricated, as heavy rail traffic would frequently dislodge the rails. The work involved hard manual labour for low pay and was normally done using shovel, crowbar, pick and hammer. Labourers were either employed by the railway or more often subcontracted by a gang leader.

112   St Pancras station views became one of London's most popular early postcards

By the turn of the twentieth century St Pancras offered an iconic image that appeared on a wide range of mass-produced postcards. These were sold by kiosks and vendors in and around the station, and were popular with both tourists and those wanting to send a quick message upon arrival or departure. Despite being common in Europe since 1870s, picture postcards only appeared in Britain in the 1890s and did not grow in popularity until the early 1900s when over a million were being posted every week. At the turn of the century, the sender was not allowed to write anything other than the recipient's address on the reverse and it took a few more years for the now familiar divided-back style to be introduced. Hundreds of cards survive from travellers passing through St Pancras, ranging from those writing home with news of their holiday to others trying to arrange a romantic rendezvous.

113   St Pancras station sold promotional puzzles and games

During the opening decades of the twentieth century the vibrant atmosphere of a bustling St Pancras platform scene depicted in 'St Pancras Going North' proved a popular advertising image for the Midland Railway and was widely reproduced in a variety of forms, including on posters, postcards, jigsaws, and, as in one case, as a lithograph print on the lid of a novelty tea caddy. The rest of the tin incorporated a series of other images, including Midland Railway steam trains travelling to Scotland, the station at Matlock and the Midland Railway Steamer that carried holidaymakers to the Isle of Man.

Mass-produced novelty railway merchandise was incredibly popular at this point, providing an important source of revenue and advertising for railway companies always looking to get one over on their rivals. From the late nineteenth century onwards, images of railway stations and locomotives became widespread subjects depicted on another popular pastime – jigsaw puzzles. Railway companies were quick to realise the merchandising and advertising potential of a growing enthusiasm for jigsaws, with the Great Western Railway commissioning over 1 million promotional jigsaws during the interwar period, many of which were sold cheaply or simply given away.

114   There has been a Christmas tree at St Pancras station since at least 1890

Throughout the late nineteenth and early twentieth centuries, St Pancras station remained a popular image depicted on many postcards. One typical example by artist David Shepherd from 1890 depicts a Christmas scene as an elite family prepares to depart the station. Uniformed porters can be seen moving their luggage, while a small child, wearing a sailor suit, speaks to a lady dressed as Mrs Claus. In the background, a large decorated Christmas tree can be seen. Travellers using the station at Christmas today will still see a large tree each year. Decorated evergreen trees became increasingly popular in Britain over the course of the nineteenth century after they were first introduced from Germany by the Royal Family.

115   The station once had its own official rat-catchers

As the adage goes, you are never more than 6ft from a rat in Britain. While this is unlikely to be true for much of the population, it appears more likely to have been the case for those working in the Somers Town Goods Yard. In 1909, W.R. Boelter estimated that there was a rat for every one of the 40 million people living in Britain. Although his estimate was in all likelihood greatly inflated, he did record that rats were especially common in railway station goods stores, with one rat-catcher at Liverpool New Street station catching 200 in one day. Contrary to Victorian claims that rat-catchers developed secret poisons to lure rats, throughout the period the most common method remained the use of arsenic or terriers. St Pancras station's dogs were

called Jill, Sally and Tiny. They worked with St Pancras's rat-catchers, Jim Forty and Alfred Greenwin. The station's rat-catchers constituted important members of the railway staff for much of its history.

116   Today the station has its own resident hawk

Keeping unwanted pigeons out of St Pancras station requires innovative solutions. Comet, a Harris' hawk, and his handler Mark Bigwood, patrol the station to scare off any nesting birds. Since the 2007 refurbishment, St Pancras station has, like many other famous London landmarks, used Harris' hawks to control the pigeon population. In an article written after accompanying Mark and his birds around the station, *The Financial Times* described it as 'like being in the shadow of a celebrity. The crowd parts; suited business travellers and children stop and stare, many hang back slyly filming him on iPhones'. Harris' hawks have become a familiar sight in the station and can be seen up to three times a week patrolling the vast expanse of the train shed.

117   WHSmith first opened in St Pancras station in 1908

Modern-day St Pancras International prides itself on being an attractive and convenient place to stop and shop. Yet the relationship between train stations and retail is by no means new. W.H. Smith & Son opened a kiosk at St Pancras station in 1908. William Henry Smith Snr. established the eponymous chain in the 1820s, opening a news reading room on The Strand and using the mail-coach system to distribute newspapers around the country. His son, also named William, expanded the business further by using the railways to distribute his newspapers with greater speed and efficiency. Keen to harness the growing popularity of railway travel for commercial benefit, from 1848 he began constructing a series of news kiosks within railway stations. This allowed Smith to build a brand renowned for providing news quickly and reliably, and ensuring travellers could purchase all necessary supplies for their journey. Selling cheap but respectable newspapers and books, Smith's kiosks soon replaced independent vendors, who were criticised for selling disreputable publications and soiled newspapers. While the Smith's relationship with railway companies has not always been smooth, their strategy initiated a commercial and cultural transformation inside train stations.

118 Taxis at St Pancras station used to park at platform level

Upon disembarking, a line of horse-drawn hansom cabs would be seen waiting to collect passengers. Engineer William Barlow designed the train shed so that cabs could enter and leave through two grand vaulted archways incorporated into the Midland Grand Hotel, thereby allowing passengers to avoid inclement weather. This continued well into the twentieth century, as London's black cabs replaced their horse-drawn counterparts.

Horse-drawn taxis on the St Pancras's concourse. (Publishers Collection)

119   Edwardian St Pancras station ran shuttle buses to London's other stations

The Midland Railway boasted that 'The traveller selecting the Midland Company for his "guide, philosopher and friend" will have no difficulty in obtaining a ticket by that route to almost any place where he wishes to be conveyed, at all events to some point well forward on his journey.'

In order to transfer 'through-booked passengers' between St Pancras and other London stations, such as Charing Cross and Victoria which offered services to the south coast and the Continent, the Midland

Railway provided a complimentary omnibus service. Liveried buses would shuttle passengers along London's roads to catch their onward train, with 'a reasonable quantity of personal baggage' carried free of charge atop the roof rack.

120   1920s transportation at St Pancras station ran on a surprising power source: electricity

By the 1920s electric vehicles were increasingly being used at St Pancras to move luggage and goods between the station, hotel, and goods yard. Vehicles were recharged from the mains supply at charging stations in the yard but tended to have short battery life, meaning that horses remained an important part of station infrastructure until the 1930s. Nevertheless, the sight of electric vehicles at stations in the early 1920s offered a reminder of the technological experimentation and advancement that the railways pioneered.

121   The different levels at St Pancras station were once connected by hydraulic lifts

Technological innovation was in evidence all around St Pancras, as planners harnessed new tools of the industrial revolution to ensure the efficient movement of goods and engines around the station complex. During the early 1920s, just in front of the station signal box, a hydraulic lift platform allowed wagons to move between the upper and lower levels of track to access the undercroft. The lift was powered through heated water, maintained at constant high pressure and propelled through iron pipes by coal-heated steam pumps. A horse would have

been used to move wagons into position as they prepared to ascend or descend. The lift was primarily used to move wagons filled with beer barrels to the level of the undercroft where they were unloaded by workmen using a system of capstans and ropes.

122   Hydraulic lifts were also used to raise and lower carriages at St Pancras station

At the turn of the twentieth century, vehicles such as 4-4-0 engine shunting coaches, parked near the St Pancras signal box, relied on a platform leading to a hydraulic lift, which allowed carriages to be moved to the lower level of track that ran into the undercroft. Despite retrospective accounts often wreathing the age of steam in a nostalgic haze, not all remembered it so fondly; one former engine driver in the 1950s recalled steam trains as 'the most horrible, dirtiest things it represented nothing but hard graft'.

123 Transport from rail to road in the Edwardian era relied on a complicated system of ramps

Once goods had travelled by rail to the Somers Town Goods Depot, they would often require onwards conveyance by road. Ramp access, running from the Depot's main entrance on the corner of Phoenix Street/Brill Place and Ossulston Street to the upper track level, allowed goods to be transferred directly across from the rail wagons to waiting carts or vans. The lower level included a series of cobbled throughways, designed to make the collection process as efficient as possible. When the railways were new, the only method of onward transportation was by horse and cart; however, this began to change with the development of first steam and then diesel-powered lorries. The first internal combustion lorry was produced in 1899, and although they were still outclassed by the railways in terms of range, by 1919 they were beginning to monopolise short and medium haul trips, particularly in wealthy urban environments such as London. They revolutionised the delivery market, allowing more to be conveyed by one worker, in a faster time and a more efficient manner. Even then, though, it wasn't until the 1930s and 40s that the motor lorry started to become capable of rivalling the railways as long-distance haulers of heavy loads.

124   The tram network around St Pancras vanished earlier than elsewhere in London

Looking down the Pentonville Road towards St Pancras station in the 1930s would have revealed a bustling scene – and also a sense of the rapid changes to London's public transport system and street life during the first decades of the twentieth century. Electric trams had been a part of London life since the first one rolled over Westminster Bridge towards Tooting in 1903. Owned and run by London County Council (LCC), they then were seen as the cheapest, fastest way of moving the masses around the city prior to the development of sufficiently powerful motorbuses. At their peak in 1914 the London tram network was the largest in Europe and a serious rival to the Underground. However, the war curbed plans for further expansion and starved them of investment. Using this, along with changing views on the inflexibility of trams, as justification, from 1935 the London Passenger Transport Board started an ambitious replacement programme using both motor and trolley buses. The trolley buses were a particularly useful asset, as they utilised the tram's existing electrification infrastructure without requiring the costly and awkward tracks set into the streets. Although trams did continue in the capital until July 1952, by the time the Second World War intervened most of the trams in North London had been replaced, including those at St Pancras.

125   St Pancras station trains used to be loaded from horse-drawn drays

Before 1939, horses were a common sight at British railway termini. In 1924, the LMS owned 10,000 horses, the same number as it had locomotives. Although horses were gradually superseded by motor vehicles after 1914, they continued to fulfil a wide range of roles at the station, including moving heavy goods between the platforms and goods yard. Porter would lead horses, drawing laden drays, along a St Pancras station platform ready to be loaded onto a train.

126   Edwardian St Pancras station was particularly marketed to American tourists

As the century drew to a close there were an ever-growing number of American tourists crossing the Atlantic, resulting in a burgeoning British tourist industry at the turn of the twentieth century. As *The Midland Railway of England* travel guide of 1902 noted, 'Americans are so accustomed to speed in their daily life that many find it difficult to "slow up" even in their times of rest, recuperating and pleasure. Hence it is a common thing for tourists landing at Liverpool to rush straight to London or Paris, closing their eyes to many of the good things they pass on the way.' The forty-page guide went on to direct passengers along 'the best route for seeing the beauties of rural England, its castle, abbeys and cathedrals, the haunts of great writers – Scott, Byron, Burns, Bunyan and Shakespeare', taking them from their docking in Liverpool to the 'shelter of St Pancras, the terminus of the Midland Railway in London, one of the finest examples of the work of Sir Gilbert Scott R.A. and the largest single span roof in the world'. Alongside detailed descriptions of sights and attractions, it offered maps, ticket and timetable information, and a list of 'some American terms and English equivalents' to ensure visitors enjoyed a smooth trip.

127   St Pancras station was originally the official departure point for the Royal Family

Until 1924, St Pancras was the principal point of departure for members of the Royal Family travelling to Wolferton, the nearest station to the Sandringham estate in Norfolk. They would travel by special train, not open to members of the public, with each journey carefully planned to ensure smooth running. A pamphlet was issued to railway staff before Edward VII and Queen Mary travelled to Norfolk early in 1905 containing detailed instructions of the timetable, route, and changes to twenty other services that had to be delayed until the Royal Train had passed.

128   A Royal honeymoon began at St Pancras station

In the summer of 1896 London celebrated the wedding of Queen Victoria's granddaughter, Princess Maud, to Prince Christian Frederik Carl Georg Valdemar Axel of Denmark, more commonly known as Prince Carl. Maud's father was the Prince of Wales, the future Edward VII, while Carl was the second son of King Frederick VIII and Louise of Denmark. Having married in an elaborate ceremony full of pomp and circumstance at the private chapel in Buckingham Palace, the couple enjoyed a banquet in the State Dining Room before travelling to St Pancras, where they boarded a special train that would carry them away to Norfolk on honeymoon. The press acclaimed Maud's popularity with Londoners, observing that excited crowds filled brightly decorated streets to cheer the open carriage along its route from Buckingham Palace to St Pancras. Although Prince Carl was not first in line to the Danish throne, he was invited in 1905 to assume the throne of Norway following the dissolution of its union with Sweden. As Queen Maud of Norway she sat alongside her husband until her death in 1938 and is buried in the royal mausoleum in Oslo.

129   King George V was once attacked at St Pancras station

Readers of the French newspaper *Le Petit Parisien* on 29 January 1923 were met by a front-page story recounting an attempted attack on the British Royal Family as they departed St Pancras after travelling from their New Year break at Sandringham. Under the headline, 'A mutilated man threatens death to the English sovereigns', the report recounted how, as King George V and his wife Queen Mary walked from the station towards their waiting car, a former serviceman, named Tommy Abrahams, jumped from a taxi where he had been hiding, brandished a crutch and shouted: 'If I had a gun, I would kill all of you!' Abrahams had lost his leg at Ypres during the First World War and was angry at his meagre army pension. According to the paper, he had been suffering from 'a nervous sickness resulting from a cerebral commotion created by an explosion' and had previously tried to approach the Royal Family to make a complaint. The report praised the King and Queen's composure, as they ignored Abrahams and continued to walk to their car before being driven away to Buckingham Palace. Although Abrahams was arrested, the article explained that his illness meant it was unlikely he would face prosecution. This perhaps explains why the incident received

King George V decorating troops, one of whom would go on to attack him at St Pancras. (Library of Congress, LC-DIG-ggbain-24634)

surprisingly little coverage in the British press. Despite David Lloyd George's promise to make a 'land fit for heroes' in the aftermath of the war, the British government never made sufficient provision for returning veterans; war pensions were low and poorly administered, while many veterans found it difficult to obtain work as businesses were not obliged to rehire employees who had left to fight. Those who had suffered debilitating injuries or were suffering from post-traumatic mental health conditions, commonly labelled at the time as 'shell shock', found this process especially difficult. To compensate for the state's shortcomings a variety of veterans' groups, including the British Legion, were founded to offer support to those, like Abrahams, who struggled to re-establish themselves in post-war society.

130   St Pancras station was the starting point for the Orient Express

Few trains have caught the public imagination like the Orient Express. The luxury service transported passengers across Europe to Istanbul. The Orient Express started in 1883 as the idea of Belgian rail entrepreneur Georges Nagelmackers. Initially, it ran from Paris to Istanbul, via Munich, Vienna and Bucharest, but later expanded to include services from London. The lavish decorations, deep leather furniture and mahogany panelling in its Pullman saloons and sleeping cars exuded opulent luxury, with the train popular amongst royalty and aristocratic elites across Europe. In the twentieth century, it has formed the setting for numerous murder mystery novels by the likes of Agatha Christie and Graham Greene, and later many films and television dramas.

131   Unusual items transported by British Rail include a statue of Britain's fattest man

As part of the celebrations for the 1981 Leicester Festival, British Rail dispatched a life-sized sculpture of Daniel Lambert, a famous inhabitant of the city and at his death in 1809 reputedly the most corpulent man in England, from St Pancras station to Leicester. The connection between the station and the city goes back to St Pancras' origins. Not only did the Midland Railway have extensive links to the city but one of the first trains to leave St Pancras on the morning of 1 October 1868 travelled to Leicester in a time of 134 minutes en route to Manchester. Lambert was born in Leicester in 1770 and later succeeded his father as the keeper of the city's gaol. Following the closure of the prison in 1805, Lambert travelled to London in a specially constructed carriage, where his weight led him to become a popular 'curiosity' within London society. Rumoured to have wrestled a bear and well-known for breeding fighting cocks, Lambert was described by a contemporary as having a manly and intelligent face but with legs like pillows that nearly buried his feet. At his death, aged just 39, he weighed 53 stone and had to be buried in a specially made coffin. He has remained a popular figure in Leicester, with the sculpture enjoying a first-class journey on his return trip.

132   Post office trains once ran through St Pancras station

St Pancras train shed saw some of the last Royal Mail's Travelling Post Office (TPO) trains. The carriage of mail by train has been a feature of railway operations since the very beginning. Indeed, wherever a railway opened any mail traffic along its route would often migrate immediately from road. The first dedicated TPO took the form of a converted horsebox, running on the Grand Junction Railway from 1838. By February 1855 the Great Western Railway was running the first dedicated mail train, including TPO vehicles. The last TPO service ran on 9 January 2004 and was formed of vehicles of this type, although dedicated mail trains do still run between London, Warrington and Glasgow merely without any sorting operation.

Many TPO vehicles also included apparatus to collect and dispatch mail on the move, allowing a greater number of destinations to be served and speeding up journey times. Initially, the post would be stored in locked compartments in the guard's van or a secure vehicle and sorted at its destination. However, as the volume of mail increased it was deemed necessary to sort post on the move. This type of sorting coach – the British Railways (BR) MK1 type, introduced from 1959, at a time when there were forty-nine TPO services running across the BR network – represented the final development of British TPOs.

133 The postmen's national one-day strike caused chaos at St Pancras station

A Post Office supervisor was ordered to guard the mounting pile of post that accumulated at St Pancras station after Britain's postal system ground to a halt during the 1964 postal strike. On 16 July, 120,000 British postal workers withdrew their labour in demand of higher pay and less overtime. The one day strike was the first official industrial action by General Post Office workers in almost seventy years. An earlier walk-out, planned for April, had been called off at the last minute after Postmaster General Reginald Bevins offered an inquiry into how postal workers' pay was calculated. But by the summer, industrial action was back on the table. The union demanded a pay increase of 10.5 per cent, but the government would concede only 4 per cent. Despite appeals to the public not to post letters, envelopes and parcels quickly piled up. In London alone, 28 million letters were waiting when postal workers returned the next day. Only after additional strike action the following week did the government budge sufficiently to satisfy the UPW, offering an immediate pay rise of 6.5 per cent.

134 The station has played a part in sporting history

In October 1934, scores of enthusiastic fans gathered at St Pancras station to witness the start of a piece of sporting history. The recipients of the crowd's adulation were the England Women's Cricket Team who, led by their captain Betty Archdale, were embarking for Australia to participate in the first ever women's Test match. The three-match series proved a success for England: they won two matches and drew the third. The entire team performed well but particular praise was reserved for England's dominant all-rounder, Myrtle Maclagan. Indeed, after the men's team had lost the Ashes series earlier that summer, enthusiasm for the women's team grew ever stronger and this fervour was pithily captured in this quatrain from the *Morning Post:* 'What matter that we lost, mere nervy men / Since England's women now play England's game / Wherefore Immortal Wisden, take your pen / And write MACLAGAN on the scroll of fame.

135 The West Indies Cricket Team departed from St Pancras station in September 1951

The tour was billed as the world championship of cricket, with both teams having beaten England during the previous eighteen months. In the event Australia won the series 4-1, but came in for criticism for their overly aggressive bowling. The group included Kenneth Rickards, Frank Worrell, Clyde Walcott, Roy Marshall and Everton Weekes. During the West Indies 1950 Test series against England, the impressive performances of Walcott, Weekes and Worrell led to them being dubbed the 'Three Ws', with Weekes named Wisden Cricketer of the year for 1951. Frank Worrell's significance, in particular, extended beyond the pitch as he stood to the fore in challenging the racial prejudice that permeated West Indian cricket in the 1950s. In 1959, he became the first person of colour to captain the West Indies Test team and following retirement in 1963 was appointed to the Jamaican Senate and Knighted.

136   Visitors to St Pancras station include the FA Cup

Following Manchester United's 3-1 FA Cup final victory over Leicester City in 1963, United captain Noel Cantwell leant out the train window with the trophy as it prepared to leave St Pancras for Manchester. Over 99,000 people watched United triumph at Wembley through goals from Denis Law and David Herd. Victory secured the club its first trophy since the Munich Air Disaster in 1958, which had killed eight of the Manchester United squad.

137   Nobel Laureates to depart from St Pancras station include Rabindranath Tagore

Born in Bengal in 1861, Rabindranath Tagore went onto establish himself as a writer, poet and philosopher of global renown. He published in both Bengali and English, and was awarded the Nobel Prize in Literature in 1913. Although Tagore was knighted in 1915, he renounced the title in 1919 following the British massacre of unarmed civilians at Jallianwala Bagh, in the city of Amritsar. He came to St Pancras station in 1931. Tagore had been visiting Britain to raise funds for an experimental school at Santiniketan, which he had help to found. While in Britain he gave a series of lectures in which he celebrated the friendship between Britain and India but stressed the need for political change. His visit coincided with the final stages of the First Round Table Conference on Indian constitutional reform, then being held in London. Tagore feared the consequences of rising nationalism in India and Europe, and in one speech to the All Peoples' Association, in London January 1931, warned that trusting politicians to run the League of Nations in the interests of peace was like utilising a band of robbers to organise the police.

Rabindranath Tagore, *c.*1916.
(Library of Congress, LC-USZ62-123106)

Sir. Rabindranath Tagore

138   St Pancras station was the official departure point for the Schools Empire Tour

Throughout the late nineteenth and early twentieth centuries various educational and charitable organisations attempted to strengthen bonds within the British empire by encouraging British children to visit colonial territories. For example, groups of schoolboys departed St Pancras for Australia as part of one such scheme, the Schools Empire Tour. This was a decidedly exclusive programme, with participation limited to white public-school boys. Founded by the headmaster of Winchester College, Dr Montague Rendall, the aim of the tours was to introduce those expected to assume positions of leadership across British society to the possibilities open to them in colonial territories and, in so doing, inculcate a sense of empire patriotism. Rendall's vision of empire was heavily racialised and paternalistic, believing that the British had a right and responsibility to govern those he assumed to be less advanced. Across twenty-two years over 500 public school boys went on the annual tour, with many subsequently taking up careers in empire themselves. Despite departing in the middle of the school year, this group spent five months touring Australia. While there they visited government house, meeting the Prime Minister, surfed off Sydney and undertook several excursions into Western Australia's outback, which included kangaroo shooting. In total they travelled 31,000 miles, including 22,000 miles at sea as they completed a full circuit of the globe travelling out across the Indian Ocean and returning via the Pacific and Atlantic. Despite its popularity amongst the public schools during the interwar years, others were less convinced that the scheme's elite focus served much use in a period described by Colonial Secretary Leo Amery, as a 'hurricane age of questioning and change'. After 1945 the tours ceased, as efforts to rebuild the empire following the ruptures of the Second World War focussed on less elitist and racially exclusive methods.

139   St Pancras station was also the starting point for thousands of child emigrés

Child and youth migration from Britain to colonial territories began in the nineteenth century and was endorsed by a variety of charitable and religious organisations. Between 1870 and 1914, some 80,000 child emigrants, also known as 'British Home Children', were sent to British colonies, mostly Australia and Canada, to start new lives. In the aftermath of the First and Second World Wars, this number rose even further with more than 130,000 children leaving Britain between the 1920s and 1970s. British children emigration initiatives had several goals: they focused on sending impoverished

British children and orphans abroad to start a new life, reducing the number of poor children in British streets and cities, and populating the former colonies. Many began their journey to Australia as part of the Catholic Emigration Scheme, which sent groups of orphaned girls from institutions such as the St Anthony's Home for Girls in Feltham to St Pancras and onwards to board a train for Tilbury docks, from where they sailed to Adelaide, South Australia, to stay with the Vincent Paul Sisters of Charity. The reality of emigration for many children was profoundly challenging and complex. Even as they left poverty behind, few had any say in their departure. Many never saw their family again and, as recent oral history projects have revealed, children could face terrible abuse in their new homes. Since 1987, the Child Migrants Trust has worked to secure a public enquiry into the child migration schemes and help reunite divided families.

Many London boys, meanwhile, bid farewell to sisters as they left St Pancras Station. Forty-one boys aged between 16 and 18 left for Australia in May 1953, for example, including Peter Bartlett of Carshalton. Peter's emigration was organised by the Big Brother Movement, a scheme founded in 1925 to take youths from Britain to work on rural farms in Australia. According to the movement's founder, Sir Richard Linton, the success of this migration policy depended on whether one could recruit boys of a high moral, physical and intellectual standard. Emigration to Australia and the other 'white Commonwealth nations' surged in the aftermath of the Second World War, with over 1 million people leaving Britain to start new lives overseas between 1946 and 1955. Many schemes were run or supported by Commonwealth governments eager to increase the number of young people arriving in their countries. In 1947, the Big Brother Movement raised £50,000 to send 'clean-living, well-mannered, British boys with grit and determination to make a career for themselves in Australia'. The movement paired 'Little Brothers' from Britain with a Big Brother in Australia. Even so, while most boys undertook arduous work on rural farms, many of their guardians remained in cities and rarely visited. Over 2,000 left for Australia with the movement before 1939 and a further 1,100 by 1953. It continued until 1982.

140   Poet Sir John Betjeman himself unveiled the train named after him at St Pancras station

At a St Pancras at a ceremony the year before his death, the station's great champion, Sir John Betjeman, unveiled a new British Rail train bearing his name. Betjeman's nostalgic love of steam railways and the Victorian age energised his campaign to save the Midland Hotel from destruction in the 1960s. Writing in *The Daily Telegraph*, he penned a series of impassioned articles that celebrated and defended the station's architectural and historical significance, with the following extract taken from a 1966 article entitled 'Temple to the Age of Steam':

To some people St Pancras is just an old station which may be replaced. To others it is an irreplaceable example of the exuberant architecture of the 1860s, when British engineers, railways and business led the world Like the Albert Memorial, St Pancras Hotel – by the same architect – and station are coming into their own. But under a British Rail plan to amalgamate St Pancras and King's Cross stations into a single modern terminus, the station and hotel are threatened with destruction and replacement by another series of biscuit boxes. Neither building is listed by the Ministry of Public Building and Works. Yet since the Doric portico at Euston – the first grand entrance to the first trunk railway in the world – was demolished, despite the offer of Mr Valori, the demolisher, to number the stones and keep them at his own expense till the portico could be re-erected on another site, there is no monument in London to the railway age comparable with St Pancras.'

On the main concourse of St Pancras International stands a fitting tribute: a statue of Sir John gazing in awe and appreciation at the great arc of the Victorian train shed roof. The 8.5ft sculpture by Martin Jennings was commissioned by London and Continental Railways during the recent station redevelopment. The statue stands on a disc inscribed with the words 'Who saved this glorious station', inviting visitors to St Pancras to share in Betjeman's delight at the station's architecture.

141   A BBC presenter once walked on the roof of St Pancras station's train shed

Appearing in an October 1970 segment for the BBC's long-running science and technology programme *Tomorrow's World*, presenter William Wollard demonstrated Herbert Stokes' 'roof shoes' invention by walking across St Pancras' sloping train shed roof. The adjustable aluminium shoes were intended to aid those working on roofs by allowing the wearer to walk upright across steep angles, whilst their sponge rubber bottoms made them useable even in the wet. Even though Stokes' invention did not take off, many of the items showcased on *Tomorrow's World* did become commonplace over the ensuing decades. In a programme two years later, Wollard presented a segment on the radical, revolutionary and, for many, improbable idea that Britain would soon be connected to mainland Europe by a tunnel that would allow travellers to leave London and be in Paris in just a couple of hours!

142   The 2012 Olympic relay began at St Pancras station

Throughout the build-up to the 2012 London Olympics, St Pancras played a prominent role in preparations. In March 2011, the then London Mayor, Boris Johnson, and Chair of the Olympic Organising Committee, Lord Coe, unveiled a set of giant Olympic rings which hung from wires attached to the train shed roof. Three months later, Lord Coe returned to begin the Olympic torch relay, which would see the torch tour the country before arriving back in London for the opening ceremony. The torch itself was triangular in shape to signify the three times London had hosted the Olympics, in 1908, 1948 and 2012. As the torch toured the country, it was carried by a succession of bearers each chosen by their local community and symbolised by the 8,000 circles crafted on the torch.

Arriving back in London the day before the London Olympics' opening ceremony on 27 July 2012, the Olympic Torch returned to St Pancas as it neared the end of its seventy-day, 8,000-mile relay around Britain. Large crowds enjoyed performances by acrobats and jazz musicians on a stage beneath the Olympic rings in preparation for the handover of the torch at 7.38 a.m. by charity worker and volunteer Danny McCubbin to Luke Corduner, a PE Teacher, who would carry the torch on its penultimate journey around Central London. The event marked the opening of a hectic fortnight for the station, as 1.4 million visitors and spectators travelled to the Olympic Park aboard the special Olympic Javelin service, which whisked passengers from St Pancras to the park in Stratford in just seven minutes.

143   The St Pancras mural has moved three times

First painted in 1984, Karen Gregory's 1452sq.ft mural emblazoned Somers Town's turbulent and transformative history over the previous 200 years onto the area's very fabric. The project was initially funded by the Greater London Council and intended to serve an educational as well as artistic purpose. The mural as seen today is in its third incarnation, following the demolition of the walls on which the previous two versions were painted. This happened first in 1993, when the writer and Somers Town historian Claire Tomalin organised a successful fundraising campaign to have the mural restored on the wall of St Mary & St Pancras Church of England Primary School, which included a petition in Parliament, and then again in 2007, when local residents voted for it to be repainted in its present location on the other side of the school in Polygon Street.

The mural charts the changing economic, social, and demographic profile of Somers Town. It depicts some of the area's famous inhabitants alongside less well-known residents, as it moves from eighteenth-century rural charm, through the privations of nineteenth-century industrialisation and onto the campaigns for better housing provision in the twentieth century. With each rendition new figures have been added, as new layers are incorporated into Somers Town's rich history.

144   The famous statue by the Eurostar terminal contains 20 tons of bronze

The 9m-tall statue, designed by Paul Day, entitled *The Meeting Place*, is located at the southern end of St. Pancras's Eurostar terminal, directly beneath the station's main clock. Constructed in 2007, at a price of approximately £1 million, it is composed of 20 tons of bronze. For Day, the statue symbolises 'something that can be universally recognised as a symbol of travel is [a] couple being reunited'.

Not only is *The Meeting Place* a meeting of persons but also of peoples, epitomising the confluence of British and French culture, and St Pancras' position as London's gateway to Europe. Around the base of the sculpture are carved intricate scenes spanning St Pancras' history. These include depictions of the construction of the railway and station, early rail passengers, troops departing for war, and commuters using the station today. In its design, the sculpture seeks to capture the moments of intimacy that have brought this space to life since 1868.

145   St Pancras station has featured in the *The Beano*

From late nineteenth-century boys' adventure stories to Richard Hannay's dash from London in John Buchan's *Thirty Nine Steps*, St Pancras station has long proved a popular setting in numerous works of fiction, cartoons and children's literature. *The Beano's* 2015 Annual, showing Dennis the Menace and Gnasher dashing to catch the Beanotown Express on its cover, illustrated another of the various ways in which the station's appeal continues to resonate today. In the run-up to Christmas 2014, the station embraced this connection with one of Britain's best-known comics, fitting the concourse with a new graphic installation, hosting an exhibition of historic Beano annual covers, and even adding a Beano theme to the station's Christmas tree.

146   The entire St Pancras Underground complex was moved in 1944

The London Underground network has been an integral part of the capital's transport infrastructure ever since the Metropolitan Railway opened the first line between Paddington and Farringdon, via what would become King's Cross St Pancras, in 1863. The station is now the second busiest on the network, with 95.03 million entries and exits across six lines in 2016. By 1925 the deep-level City & South London Railway and the Piccadilly Railway, later the Bank branch of the Northern Line and the Piccadilly Line respectively, were in place. The two deep-level tube lines arrived at St Pancras forty-three years after the Metropolitan in 1906 and 1907. However, due to the lines being owned by rival private companies, the stations were kept separate from the Metropolitan Line until the formation of the London Passenger Transport Board in 1933. The entire complex was rebuilt in 1944 to move the Metropolitan platforms 400m further west, thereby allowing better interchange with the deep-level lines and forming the basis of today's station.

147   *The Evening Standard* once described St Pancras station as 'one of London's finest – and dirtiest – Victorian buildings'

Blackened by over a century's worth of soot and dirt, by the mid 1970s St Pancras station and the Midland Hotel (then used as British Railway offices) were in dire need of cleaning. When a 4ft chunk of cast iron fell off the roof, smashed through the glass roof and landed on the floor of the ticket office in 1978, it became equally clear that the station building also required extensive conservation work.

Writing in *The Guardian*, Alan Rusbridger described the severe corrosion of iron and stone work, damaged cornless, eroded pillars, defective brickwork, and a dirty grey grease that had covered the pink and cream façade. The mammoth clean-up and restoration project started in 1976 and continued into the early 1980s at a cost of over £500,000. The restoration team used an alkaline cleaning agent and high-pressure water hoses to expose the wealth of intricate detail on the exterior of Scott's hotel, which had been rendered invisible behind encrusted layers of grime. Although prepared to acknowledge that the clean-up operation revealed the building's architectural delights, Alan Rusbridger of *The Guardian* remained perplexed as to the bigger question of what use the building should ultimately be put to, as he saw little future for it as either British Rail offices or a hotel.

Alongside teams of trained professional cleaners, a group of six teenagers were also given the opportunity to be involved in the clean-up project through a National Association of Youth Clubs' initiative called the Community Industry Project, which sought to employ disadvantaged young people. With youth unemployment rising rapidly in the mid-1970s, the scheme aimed to train and equip teenagers who had left school at age 16, with few or no formal qualifications, with useful skills. Working in association with the Greater London Council, the boys were paid for their efforts, earning between £27 and £30 per week, although this worked out at around 60 per cent lower than the average gross weekly wage in 1977.

148   St Pancras station was nearly demolished in the 1960s

As British Railways sought to reduce expenditure by rationalising London's train stations, it looked likely that St Pancras station would be demolished or merged with an expanded King's Cross. Over the ensuing decade a tense battle for the station's future played out in the press and across Whitehall.

A cartoon featuring St Pancras, drawn by the famous political caricaturist William Papas (1927–2000) to accompany an article by Norman Shrapnel, appeared in *The Guardian* newspaper in 1962, under the headline 'The Railway Cathedral'. Papas captures the imposing dimensions and grandeur of the Midland Grand's Victorian architecture, which appears as a slightly incongruous backdrop to the busy street scene on the Euston Road. In his article, Shrapnel followed a similar line:

> People never live up to a cathedral, and St Pancras is a cathedral of sorts. It needs dramatic weather to set it off: a day of swirling cloud, a lurid sunset,

best of all a heavy snowstorm. We know then how insignificant we are. Watching tiny figures swathed in scarves struggling against the storm – this is probably the only building so immense that there is actually heavy weather inside it – you appreciate how puny is Man, and how mighty was rail in the heyday before Mr Beeching cut it to size. This great railhead, this mystical marriage of art and function in Byzantine-Gothic form, surely stands among the world's most monstrous and wonderful buildings.

Shrapnel continued to laud the building's architectural and historical significance in elegiac tones but, at a time when St Pancras' future remained shrouded in uncertainty, concluded by stating, 'if St Pancras is a dream, King's Cross is certainly the awakening.' Ultimately, the dreamers won out and the station was granted Grade I listed status in 1967.

149   There was nearly another station at St Pancras

By the mid 1980s there was growing enthusiasm amongst planners and government officials for a radical redevelopment of the area around St Pancras. A120-acre site was identified in 1988 by the London Regeneration Corporation for a multi-million-pound overhaul. It proposed building a new international railway station diagonally beneath King's Cross Station and a series of new office buildings to the north of the stations. As had been the case in the 1860s, the project required an Act of Parliament to be authorised but, despite initial enthusiasm, by 1992 it appeared increasingly unfeasible. Engineering problems, a decline in the demand for office space, and rising costs led John Major's Conservative government to seek alternative options for regeneration, including one that proposed bringing Channel Tunnel trains directly into St Pancras.

150 There is a Lego St Pancras station

Made from over 120,000 bricks and standing 5ft tall, a remarkable recreation of St Pancras station and hotel in Lego was built by professional Lego builder Warren Elsmore. It took Warren more than 500 hours and over two years to complete and incorporates wonderful attention to detail: passengers can be seen running to catch working models of Eurostar trains, whilst police patrol the platforms and diners sit at the station's champagne bar. In 2013 it was displayed in Waterstones Piccadilly for a month and has since toured various conventions and exhibitions. Warren writes about the process of recreating St Pancras station in his book *Brick City*.

REFERENCES

'The Architect and Building News, Volume 4', *The Architect*, 16 July 1870

'Arrival of War Refugees', *The Times*, 17 May 1940

Clarissa W. Atkinson, '"A Pride in Being West Indian": Claudia Jones and The West Indian Gazette', paper given at the Organization of American Historians conference in Washington DC, 2012: https://oldestvocation.wordpress.com/a-pride-in-being-west-indian-claudia-jones-and-the-west-indian-gazette/

Patricia August, 'The London Blitz: Somers Town', BBC WW2 People's War, 11 February 2004: http://www.bbc.co.uk/history/ww2peopleswar/stories/94/a2287794.shtml

Ernest Aves, Notebook: Police District 18 (Somers Town and Camden Town), 1898/98, Charles Booth Archive, London School of Economics, BOOTH/B/356

'Bad Railways? Blame it on the 1950s', BBC News Online, 16 May 2002: http://news.bbc.co.uk/1/hi/uk/1989357.stm

Alfred Barnard, *The Noted Breweries of Great Britain and Ireland*, vols 1 and 2 (London: Sir Joseph Causton & Sons, 1889)

E.G. Barnes, *The Midland Main Line: 1875–1922* (London: Allen Unwin, 1969)

Edward Barrett Warman, *Indian Club Exercises* (New York: American Sports Publishing Company, 1913)

Derrick Baxby, 'Edward Jenner (1749–1823)', in *Oxford Dictionary of National Biography*

'The Beano Annual 2015 celebrates chart topping success', DC Thompson Press Release, 9 January 2015: https://www.dcthomson.co.uk/2015/01/the-beano-annual-2015-celebrates-chart-topping-success/

Hilary Beckles, 'The Political Ideology of West Indies Cricket Culture', in Hilary Beckles and Brian Stodart (eds), *Liberation Cricket: West Indies Cricket Culture* (Manchester: Manchester University Press, 1995)

R. Bell, *History of the British Railways During the War, 1939–45*, (London: Railway Gazette, 1946)

'Belle de nos jours', *The Guardian*, 2 May 2004: https://www.theguardian.com/film/2004/may/02/biography.features

Luis Angel Bernardo y Garcia and Matthew Buck, 'Belgian society in exile: an attempt at a synthesis', in Martin Conway & José Gotovich, *Europe in Exile: European Exile Communities in Britain, 1940–1945* (New York: Berghahn Books, 2001)

John Betjeman, 'Temple to the Age of Steam', *Daily Telegraph*, 11 November 1966

'The Big Brother Movement', *The Times*, 15 January 1947

The Birmingham Mail, 4 June 1945

W.R. Boelter, *The Rat Problem* (London: Bale and Danielsson, 1909)

Tom Bolton, 'From Cripplegate to Agar Town: Inside London's Vanished Neighbourhoods', *The Guardian,* 24 June 2015

Charles Booth (ed.), *Life and Labour of the People in London*, vol. 2 (London: Macmillan & Co., 1892)

Bomb Sight: http://bombsight.org/#15/51.5050/-0.0900

Simon Bradley, *St Pancras Station*, (London: Profile Books, 2010)

Simon Bradley, *The Railways: Nation, Network & People* (London: Profile Books, 2016)

'British Postal Strike Halts Mail', *The New York Times*, 17 July 1964

The Builder, 30 March 1878, quoted in Jack Simmons, *St Pancras Station* (London: Historical Publications Ltd, 2012)

The Bystander, 29 October 1924

Cambridge Independent Press, 29 June 1900

Duncan Campbell-Smith, *Masters of the Post: the Authorized History of the Royal Mail* (London: Penguin, 2011)

Richard Cavendish, 'The First WH Smith Railway Bookstall', *History Today*, 48:11, November 1998

Elton Chan, Caroline Freisfeld & Ana Villarreal Anzaldo, 'Social Infrastructure: The Regeneration of Somers Town', *LSE Cities,* 2016

'Chancellor Fails to Avert Postal Strike', *The Guardian*, 16 July 1964

'Charges After St Pancras May Day Rally', *The Times*, 2 May 1958

'Child emigration', National Museums Liverpool: https://www.liverpoolmuseums.org.uk/maritime/archive/sheet/10

Deborah Cohen, *The War Come Home: Disabled Veterans in Britain and Germany, 1914–1939* (Berkeley: University of California Press, 2001)

Barry Coldrey, 'The Big Brother Movement – Good British Stock: Child and Youth Migration to Australia' (Canberra: National Archives of Australia, 1999)

The Complete Railway Traveller 1903 (London, 1903), The National Archives, RAIL/491/1083

G.C. Cook, *From Greenwich Hulks to Old St Pancras* (Bloomsbury: Bloomsbury Publishing, 2015)

Daily Herald, 18 February 1939

Daily Herald, 25 May 1939

Daily Mirror, 30 September 1944

'Deadlock at the Post Office', *The Guardian*, 15 July 1964

'Demolishing Slums by Dynamite', *The Times*, 24 January 1930

Steven Denford and F. Peter Woodward (eds), *Streets of St Pancras, Somers Town and The Railway Lands* (London: Camden History Society, 2002)

Steven L.J. Denford, *Agar Town: The Life and Death of a Victorian 'Slum'* (London: Camden History Society, 1995)

Paul Dobraszczyk, *Iron, Ornament and Architecture in Victorian Britain: Myth and Modernity, Excess and Enchantment* (Abingdon: Routledge, 2017)

Jan Dobrzynski, *British Railway Tickets* (London: Shire Publications, 2013)

'Dogs to be Pre-Paid: Order Number 31', 9 November 1854. The National Archives, RAIL/491/828.

Alf Dole and Jeff Hudson, *The Pearly Prince of St Pancras* (London: Simon & Schuster, 2014)

The Drinking Fountain Association, 'The Metropolitan Drinking Fountain and Cattle Trough Association': http://www.drinkingfountains.org/Attachments(PDF)/DFA%20HIstory.pdf

'Duke of Kent in Somers Town', *The Times*, 8 March 1939

Dundee Evening Telegraph, 28 October 1932

'Early Day Motion, sponsored by Frank Dobson MP: Somers Town Mural', 8 March 1993: http://www.parliament.uk/edm/1992-93/1544

David Edgerton, *Shock of the Old: Technology and Global History Since 1900* (London: Profile Books, 2011)

W.E. Edwards, 'How Trains are Controlled: VI – The Signals at St Pancras', *Railway Magazine*, November 1905

'Electricity on the Midland Railway', *Leicester Chronicle*, 4 February 1899

Walter Everett, *The Beatles as Musicians: Revolver Through The Anthology,* (Oxford: Oxford University Press, 1999)

David Hugh Farmer, *The Oxford Dictionary of Saints* (Oxford: Oxford University Press, 2011)

Dawn Foster, interview with Steve Denholm, *Between the Tracks: The Spirit of Somers Town*, Issue 1, 2016: http://www.communitymediagroup.org.uk/downloads/publications/somers-town-1.pdf

Michael J Freeman, *Railways and the Victorian Imagination,* (New Haven: Yale University Press)

David J. Froggatt, *Railway Buttons, Badges & Uniforms* (Shepperton: Ian Allan Ltd, 1986)

Donald L. Foley, *Governing the London Region: Reorganization and Planning in the 1960s* (Berkeley: University of California Press, 1972)

'Fountain in St Pancras Old Church Gardens': https://memorialdrinkingfountains.wordpress.com/2013/11/16/st-pancras-old-church-gardens/

'Fun's Guide to London', *Fun*, 15 October 1879

Ian Gazeley, 'Women's Pay in British Industry During the Second World War', *Economic History Review*, 61:3, 2008

Dion Georgiou, '"Only a Local Affair"? Imagining and Enacting Locality through London's Boer War Carnivals', *Urban History* 45:1, February 2018

George Godwin, *Another Blow for Life* (London: Wm H. Allen & Co., 1864)

Justin Gowers, 'A fitting tribute to Betjeman', *The Guardian*, 22 July 2007

The Graphic, 29 July 1896

'Great Festival 2016', START: http://somerstownart.org/2016/07/11/great-festival-2016/

Edward Greenfield, 'Sir Alec Still a Very Fourteenth Earl', *The Guardian*, 1 October 1964

The Guardian, 24 November 1977

'The Guards Return', *The Times*, 26 February 1919

Peter Hall, *Great Planning Disasters* (Berkeley: University of California Press, 1982)

Hampshire Telegraph and Sussex Chronicle, 28 July 1894

Rosemary Harris, 'Interpreting Teenage Inter-ethnic Violence', in Tim Allen & John Eade (eds), *Divided Europeans: Understanding Ethnicities in Conflict* (The Hague: Kluwer Law International, 1999)

David Hayes, 'A History of Camden Town 1895–1914' in Helena Bonett, Ysanne Holt and Jennifer Mundy (eds), *The Camden Town Group in Context*, (London: Tate Research Publication, 2012)

Ambrose Heal, 'The Old Farm House in Tottenham Court Road', *The Spectator*, 18 October 1913

Christopher Hibbert, Ben Weinreb, John Keay, & Julia Keay, 'Tottenham Court Road', in *The London Encyclopedia* (London: Macmillan, 2010)

'History of Somers Town Mural: A Local History that Doesn't Seem to Die!', London Mural Preservation Society: http://www.londonmuralpreservationsociety.com/murals/history-somers-town-mural/

'Holborn Elects Mrs Jeger', *The Times*, 20 November 1953

'Home – And No Place Like It', *Daily Herald*, 5 June 1945

'Home at Last – It Was Their First Kiss in Three Years', *Sunday People*, 3 December 1944

'Homes For Aged Sick', *The Times*, 22 June 1951

Tony Howard, 'Let Robeson Sing': http://www2.warwick.ac.uk/services/library/mrc/explorefurther/images/robeson/

The Illustrated London News, 29 July 1896

Emma Jacobs, 'One Man's Flight From the City', *The Financial Times*, 5 December 2013

Tanya Jackson, *British Rail: The Nation's Railway* (Stroud: The History Press, 2013)

Avery Jones, 'Letters to the Editor of The Times: Catering in Hospitals', *The Times*, 11 February 1957

James Jupp, *The English in Australia*, (Cambridge: Cambridge University Press, 2004)

John R. Kellett, *The Impact of Railways on Victorian* Cities, (Abingdon: Routledge, 2014)

Kenneth Kolson, *Big Plans: The Allure and Folly of Urban Design* (Baltimore: The Johns Hopkins University Press, 2001)

Aleks Krotoski, *Hidden Histories of the Information Age*, BBC Radio 4 January 2016: http://www.bbc.co.uk/programmes/b04m3bcc

'Lady Jeger', *The Telegraph*, 16/03/2007

Henry Lake, 'The Midland Railway and its Hotels', *Belgravia: A London Magazine*, 7 October 1875

Alastair Lansley, *The Transformation of St Pancras Station* (London: Laurence King, 2012)

Keith Laybourn, *The General Strike of 1926* (Manchester: Manchester University Press, 1993)

Charles E. Lee, 'St Pancras Station, 1868–1968: Part 2', *Railway Magazine*, October 1968

'Lego Landmarks: Warren Elsmore's Brick City Exhibition Opens', *BBC News*, 17 October 2015: http://www.bbc.co.uk/news/uk-england-nottingham-shire-34543758

Hana Lewis, 'Somers Town Goods Yard: Excavations at Brill Place, Camden NW1', *London Archaeologist*, 13:11, 2014

Janet Likeman, *Nursing at University College Hospital, London 1862–1948: From Christian Vocation to Secular Profession*, unpublished PhD thesis, Institute of Education, University of London (2002): http://eprints.ioe.ac.uk/20394/1/Likeman%2C%20Janet_Redacted.pdf.

Liverpool Mercury, 27 July 1894

Liverpool Mercury, 28 July 1894

London Gardens Online: http://www.londongardensonline.org.uk/gardens-online-record.php?ID=CAM103

'London's Two By-Elections', *The Guardian*, 10 November 1953

'Lovers' Statue Installed at Eurostar Terminal', *London Evening Standard*, 22 October 2007

Peter McGough, 'The Olympia Wasn't Always Top Dog: How 1971 Changed Everything', Muscular Development, 13 August 2015: http://www.musculardevelopment.com/news/the-mcgough-report/14513-the-olympia-wasn-t-always-top-dog-how-1971-changed-everything.html

Dominic Malcolm, *Globalizing Cricket: Englishness, Empire and Identity* (London: Bloomsbury, 2012)

Rosa Matheson, *Women and The Great Western Railway* (Stroud: The History Press, 2007)

David Mathieson, *Radical London in the 1950s* (Stroud: Amberley Publishing, 2016)

'The Meeting Place', BBC News Online, 24/9/2014: http://www.bbc.co.uk/london/content/articles/2007/10/10/paul_day_stpancras_feature.shtml

Midland Railway Company construction contacts, The National Archives, RAIL/491/411-12, cited in Jack Simmons, *St Pancras Station* (London: Historical Publications Ltd, 2012)

'Midland Railway Company miscellaneous books and records, 1916–1918: a file of circulars and instructions relating to raids by hostile aircraft', The National Archives, RAIL/491/812.

Midland Railway Company, *Pocket Guide to the Midland Railway of England* (Derby: Bemrose, 1894)

Midland Railway, 'Fares from St Pancras (1911)', The National Archives, RAIL/491/764

'The Midland Railway Metropolitan Terminus, and the new line to Bedford', *The London Journal*, 24 October 1868

Midland Railway 'Notice to Staff: Recruiting', 11 September 1914, The National Archives, RAIL/491/828

Midland Railway, *The Midland Railway of England* (New York: Frank Presbrey & Co., 1902)

'The Midland Railway Works, Euston Road', *Illustrated London News*, 15 February 1868

Frederick Miller, *Saint Pancras, Past and Present: Being Historical, Traditional and General Notes of the Parish, Including Biographical Notices of Inhabitants Associated with its Topographical and General History* (London: A. Heywood & Son, 1874)

'Minutes 2949 & 2985: St Pancras Hotel Air Raid, February 17th 1918', Midland Railway Hotels & Refreshment Rooms Committee minute book, The National Archives, RAIL/491/272

'Mr Wilson's secret weapon', *The Guardian*, 1 October 1964

'Monthly Weather Report of the Meteorological Office', wol. 60, no. 12, December 1943: http://www.metoffice.gov.uk/binaries/content/assets/mohippo/pdf/f/s/dec1943.pdf

Multi-year station exit and entry figures, Transport for London, March 2017

Un mutilé menace de mort les souverains anglais', *Le Petit Parisien*, 29 January 1923: http://gallica.bnf.fr/ark:/12148/bpt6k6052791/f1.itemNational Archives, RAIL/491/774

'News in Brief: M.P.'s Widow to Contest By-Election', *The Times*, 19 October 1953

Nottingham Evening Post, 9 November 1908

'Obituary: Baroness Jeger', *The Guardian*, 7 March 2007
'Obituary of John Allen McDonald', *Minutes of the Proceedings of the Institution of Civil Engineers*, vol. 159, 1905
'One-day Postal Strike on Thursday', *Guardian*, 11 July 1964
L. O'Brien, 'Daniel Lambert (1770–1809)', *Oxford Dictionary of National Biography*
'Our Rambler at St Pancras Terminus', *The Architect*, 6 February 1869
'Olgur Lehmann Bunker Murals', BBC Wiltshire: http://www.bbc.co.uk/wiltshire/content/articles/2009/04/06/olga_lehmann_bunker_murals_feature.shtml

Samuel Palmer, *St Pancras: Being Antiquarian Topographical and Biographical Memoranda Relating to the Extensive Metropolitan Parish of St Pancras* (London: Samuel Palmer, Field and Tuer, 1870)
Michael Parkes, 'Somers Town: The Planning and Housing Crisis in London's Gold Belt', OurCity.London, 3 February 2017: http://www.ourcity.london/case-studies/guest-post-somers-town-planning-housing-crisis-londons-gold-belt/
Charles T. Pearce, *Vital statistics. Small-pox & vaccination in the United Kingdom of Great Britain and Ireland and continental countries and cities*, (London: E.W. Allen, 1882)
Simon Pepper, 'Ossulston Street: Early LCC Experiments in High-Rise Housing, 1925–29', *The London Journal*, 7, 1981
David Platt, *Steam Trains and Jigsaw Puzzles* (Bloomington: AuthorHouse UK Ltd, 2013)
'Popular Pastimes and Entertainment During the Second World War', Imperial War Museum: http://www.iwm.org.uk/history/popular-pastimes-and-entertainment-in-the-second-world-war
'Postal Dispute Ended in Britain', *New York Times*, 25 July 1964
'Postmen's Strike Called Off', Guardian, 15 April 1964
'Postmen Back to Overtime Ban', *Times*, 17 July 1964

The Railway Gazette, 13 december 1957
'Register book for Casual Small Pox Patients', London Metropolitan Archive, H/NW/1/SP/003/1.
'£200,000 return of the Pink Pancras', *Guardian*, 2 August 1977
Randy Roach, *Muscles, Smoke & Mirrors*, vol. 2 (Bloomington: AuthorHouse, 2011)
Jeffrey Richards, *The Age of the Dream Palace: Cinema and Society in 1930s Britain* (London: I.B. Tauris, 2010)

John Richardson, 'The St Pancras Affair', *Camden History Review*, vol. 2, 1974

J. R Howard Roberts and Godfrey, 'Tottenham Court Road (east side)', in *Survey of London: Vol. 21, The Parish of St Pancras Part 3: Tottenham Court Road and Neighbourhood*, London, 1949: *British History Online* http://www.british-history.ac.uk/survey-london/vol21/pt3/pp75-76

G. Roberts, 'St Pancras: Victorian "Cathedral of the Railways"', *Proceedings of the Institute of Civil Engineers: Engineering History and Heritage*, 162:3, 2009

'The Romance of Modern London', *The English Illustrated Magazine*, No. 117, June 1893

Alan Rusbridger, 'Fresh Face for a Railway Cathedral', *The Guardian*, 12 September 1979

Dominic Sandbrook, *State of emergency: Britain 1970–74* (London: Penguin, 2011)

'School of Hospital Catering', King Edward's Hospital Fund for London, 1953: http://archive.kingsfund.org.uk/3383/

The Scotsman, 9 January 1931

Norman Shrapnel, 'The Railway Cathedral', *Guardian*, 28 March 1962

Geoffrey Sherington, '"A Better Class of Boy": The Big Brother Movement, Youth Migration and Citizenship of Empire', *Australian Historical Studies*, 33:120 2002

Jack Simmons, *St Pancras Station* (London: Historical Publications Ltd, 2012)

The Sketch, 30 May 1900

Mike Simpson, *A Handbook of Indian Club Swinging* (Sheffield: Strategy Games Limited, 2009)

Frederick Smeeton Williams, *The Midland Railway: Its Rise and Progress* (London: Strahan & Company, 1876)

'Slum clearance in St Pancras', *The Times*, 30 January 1931

Bill Smith, 'The Evacuees, part 1', BBC WW2 People's War, 6 May 2005: http://www.bbc.co.uk/history/ww2peopleswar/stories/10/a4015810.shtml

Kevin Smith, 'Public transport: Another London Olympic Success', *International Railway Journal*: http://www.railjournal.com/index.php/blogs/kevin-smith/public-transport-another-london-olympic-success.html

Somers Town Action Group, In Place of Derelict Rail Land: What Somers Town Wants and Why (1974), The National Archives, AN/169/925

J. Stern & M Williams, The Essential Wisden: An Anthology of 150 Years of Wisden Cricketers' Almanack (London: Bloomsbury, 2017)

'St Francis Flats Opened', *The Times*, 15 October 1932

St Pancras Station Cleaning Grant, London Metropolitan Archives, GLC/AR/HB/02/0771/OB CG

'St Pancras Gets a Red Face Again', *Evening Standard*, 1 December 1977

'St Pancras Old Church', Parish of Old St Pancras: http://posp.co.uk/st-pancras-old-church/

'St Pancras Old Church', *Time Out*, 11 October 2013

Steven P. Swenson, 'Mapping Poverty in Agar Town: Economic Conditions Prior to the Development of St. Pancras Station in 1866', *London School of Economics Working Papers on The Nature of Evidence: How Well Do 'Facts' Travel?*, 9:6, 2006

Gareth Stedman Jones, Outcast London: A Study in the Relationship Between Classes in Victorian Society (Oxford: Oxford University Press, 1971)

'A Summertime Celebration of Culture and Art in Somers Town', *Camden New Journal*, 8 July 2010: http://archive.camdennewjournal.com/news/2010/jul/summertime-celebration-culture-and-art-somers-town

Matthew Symonds, 'Shadow of St Pancras: excavating the Age of Steam', *Current Archaeology*, Issue 256, June 2011

Tom Templeton, 'The Golden Jubilee Index 1977–2002', *The Observer*, 2 June 2002

Robert Thorne, 'St Pancras revived', in Jack Simmons, *St Pancras Station* (London: Historical Publications Ltd, 2012)

'Three Candidates to Contest Holborn By-Election', *The Guardian*, 11 November 1953

The Times, 12 May 1941

John Timbs, *The Leisure Hour: A Family Journal of Instruction and Recreation*, issue 1140, 1873

The Times, 21 November 1866

D.T. Timins, 'Notable Railway Stations: No. 19 – St Pancras', *The Railway Magazine*, June 1902

Selina Todd, *The People: The Rise and Fall of the Working Class, 1910–2010*, (London: John Murray, 2015)

Claire Tomalin, 'The Broader Picture: The Loss of a Local History', *The Independent*, 13 December 1992

Tomorrow's World: Review of the 1970s, BBC, 27 December 1979, http://www.bbc.co.uk/archive/tomorrowsworld/8019.shtml

'Violent Attack on the Tories', *The Times*, 12 November 1953

George A. Wade, 'Famous Railway Stations', *English Illustrated Magazine*, March 1900

Edward Walford, *Old and New London,* various vols (London: Cassell, Petter & Galpin, 1878)

Harry Wallop, 'St Pancras: Who Says Lego is Just Child's Play?', *Daily Telegraph*, 6 May 2013

Geri Walton, 'Child Rat Catchers of the Victorian Era': https://www.geriwalton. com/child-rat-catchers-of-victorian-era/

Wash up and Brush up, British Transport Films, 1953

David Wilcox, 'British Library hold-up hits homes', *The Evening Standard*, 17 February 1975

Charles Wilson, *First with the News: History of WH Smith 1792–1972* (London: Jonathan Cape Ltd, 1985)

Jay Winter, 'Migration, War and Empire: The British Case', *Annales de démographie historique*, 1:63, 2002

Anthony S. Wohl, *The eternal slum: housing and social policy in Victorian London* (London: Edward Arnold, 1977)

Helena Wojtczak, *Railway Women: Exploitation, Betrayal and Triumph in the Workplace* (Hastings: The Hastings Press, 2005)

Robin Woolven, 'Between Destruction and Reconstruction: London's Debris Clearance and Repair Organisation 1939–1945', in Mark Clapson & Peter J. Larkham (eds), *The Blitz and its Legacy: Wartime Destruction to Post-War Reconstruction* (Abingdon: Routledge, 2016)

G. Wright, St Pancras Labour Party, to Trades Union Council, 10 May 1926, London Metropolitan Archive: http://www.unionhistory.info/generalstrike/ Display.php?irn=5000666&QueryPage=..%2FAdvSearch.php

Yorkshire Evening Post, 1 June 1953

Yorkshire Evening Post, 9 January 1931

150 St Pancras INTERNATIONAL

Since 1868

The History Press

The destination for history
www.thehistorypress.co.uk